SOUTH INDIAN BUDDHIST ANTIQUITIES

ARCHAEOLOGICAL SURVEY OF INDIA
NEW IMPERIAL SERIES VOLUME XV

SOUTH INDIAN BUDDHIST ANTIQUITIES

INCLUDING THE

STUPAS OF BHATTIPROLU, GUDIVADA, AND GHANTASALA AND OTHER ANCIENT SITES

IN THE

KRISHNA DISTRICT, MADRAS PRESIDENCY;

WITH NOTES ON

DOME CONSTRUCTION; ANDHRA NUMISMATICS; AND MARBLE SCULPTURE

BY
ALEXR, REA, M.R.A.S.
SUPERINTENDENT ARCHAEOLOGICAL SURVEY, MADRAS

GYAN

Published by

GYAN

Gyan Publishing House
5, Ansari Road
Daryaganj, New Delhi-110002
Phone: 011-47034999, 9811692060
E-mail: books@gyanbooks.com

Distribution Network
gyanbooks.com
India, USA, Canada, UK, Australia, France

ISBN : 978-81-212-4047-5 (PB)
First Published, 1894

2nd Impression 2020

Printed at: Gyan Press, Delhi.

ARCHÆOLOGICAL SURVEY OF INDIA.

NEW IMPERIAL SERIES, VOLUME XV.

SOUTH INDIAN BUDDHIST ANTIQUITIES;

INCLUDING THE

STÛPAS OF BHAṬṬIPRÔḶU, GUḌIVÂḌA, AND GHAṆṬAŚÂLÂ. AND OTHER ANCIENT SITES

IN THE

KṚISHṆA DISTRICT, MADRAS PRESIDENCY;

WITH NOTES ON

DOME CONSTRUCTION; ANDHRA NUMISMATICS; AND MARBLE SCULPTURE.

BY

ALEXR. REA, M.R.A.S.,

SUPERINTENDENT, ARCHÆOLOGICAL SURVEY, MADRAS.

MADRAS:

PRINTED AND PUBLISHED BY THE SUPERINTENDENT, GOVERNMENT PRESS.

CALCUTTA—THACKER, SPINK & Co. BOMBAY—THACKER & Co., LD.

LONDON—TRÜBNER & Co.; B. QUARITCH; AND W. H. ALLEN & Co.

LEIPZIG—OTTO HARRASSOWITZ.

1894.

RELICS FROM THE CASKETS.

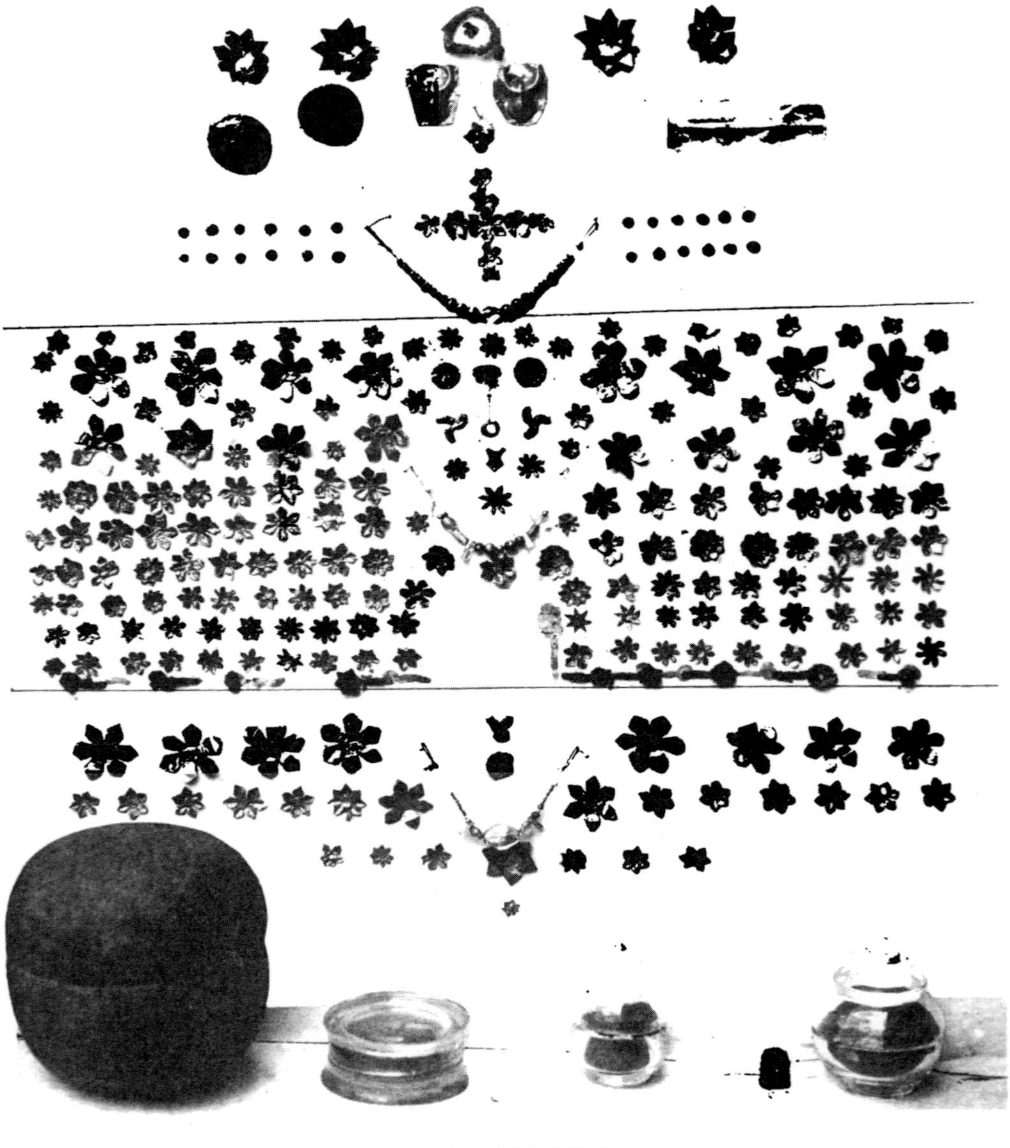

Scale, half of the Originals.

Photo-etching.

Survey of India Offices. Calcutta. December 1893.

PREFACE.

THE present volume contains the results of excavations conducted at the ruined stûpas at Bhaṭṭiprôḷu, Guḍivâḍa and Ghaṇṭaśâlâ during the beginning of 1892.

It is to be regretted that all these works, in common with most others of their class, have suffered at the hands of those who required material for the construction of roads or other such works. Though among the oldest existing monuments of an ancient civilization, their great antiquity was no protection from the despoiling hands of the adjacent villager, who scrupled not to destroy the finest works of art to provide material for the building of his wretched mud shrine. These despoilers were only gradual in their operations, as some examples which have existed up to the present time show; and, had they been the only ones, much more of these buildings might even yet have existed; but unfortunately there were others less excusable, who systematically reduced these buildings as they would a quarry. It was thought that this species of vandalism was only practised before the historical and artistic value of these ancient works was appreciated; but even yet, in spite of Government orders to the contrary, we occasionally hear of it. Such being the case, we can only unearth and endeavour to piece together such remains as have escaped the notice of the despoilers. We have been able to gather from these—in many cases seemingly shapeless mounds—that the architectural works of the Buddhists have never been excelled by any of later date existing in India. Unlike the later architecture of the Dravidians, their buildings not only contained master-pieces of detail, but the buildings were themselves perfect examples of architectural composition.

The most important results of the excavations were achieved at the former of these stûpas. These show what may still lie buried in buildings which have seemingly been denuded of everything valuable. This temple had been examined and declared utterly ruined, with nothing of value in it left; yet buried in the centre of the masonry were important historical documents in a form of alphabet hitherto unknown. Independent of the importance of the inscriptions themselves, their position in the building fixes them as an infallible index to the date of its foundation. Inscriptions placed around a building may have been engraved at or subsequent to its erection, but there can be no doubt as to these.

Regarding the character of these recently discovered inscriptions, which are written in a new variety of the Southern Maurya or Lât alphabet, Dr. Bühler writes:*

"The Bhaṭṭiprôḷu inscriptions cannot be placed later than 200 B.C., and may even be a little older. If this estimate is correct, their characters prove (what, indeed, is also made probable by facts connected with Aśoka's edicts) that during the third century B.C. several well-marked varieties of the Southern Maurya alphabet existed. For they contain a perfectly worked-out system, which cannot have sprung up in a short time, but must have had a long history.

"The importance of this result lies herein, that it removes one of the favorite arguments of those scholars who believe the introduction of writing into India to have taken place during the rule of the Maurya dynasty or shortly before its beginning. It has been stated repeatedly that one of the facts, proving the Aśoka edicts to belong to the first attempts of the Hindus in the art of writing, is the absence of local varieties among the letters of versions incised at places between which lie distances of more than a thousand miles. This argument is based, as I have pointed out more than once, on imperfect observation; and it may be met also by the obvious objection, that Aśoka's edicts were all issued from the same office, and that the importance naturally attributed to the writing of the royal clerks at Pâṭaliputra might be expected to influence the copyists in the provinces, and to induce them to imitate as closely as possible the shape of the letters used at head-quarters. Nevertheless, if the Bhaṭṭiprôḷu inscriptions now show a system of writing, which, in some respects, is radically different, and which may be reasonably supposed to be coeval with that in Aśoka's edicts, they furnish a very great help to those who, like myself, believe the art of writing to have been practised in India for centuries before the accession of Chandragupta to the throne of Pâṭaliputra."

The great majority of the mounds hitherto examined are situate in the Kṛishṇa district, where numerous unexplored remains yet exist. But as this district marks the southern boundary of the districts which ought to be rich in Buddhist remains, we may expect to make even more interesting discoveries when those to the north of it are explored. The rock-cut monuments at Nâgalapalle, and the more recently discovered remains of stûpas and monastic buildings at Arugôlu in the Godávari district, are examples of what may be expected. The latter were brought to notice by Mr. Higgens, the Collector of Godávari, who, appreciating the importance of these remains, ordered that their destruction to provide bricks should cease.

When these mounds are catalogued under the orders of Government, we will have some record of what really exists and know exactly where to go to

* *Academy*, 28th May 1892.

them. At present, without a knowledge of their locality, much time will be wasted in searching for them, and even then, some would be certain to escape notice. When this is done, we may expect less instances of dismantling of these ruins to occur; cases which being carried out in unknown localities are probably never heard of, or, if so, only after irreparable damage has been done.

It has not been thought necessary to include any historical notes on the Andhra dynasty whose works these are. All present available information on the subject has been utilized by Dr. Burgess in his recent work on Amarâvati.

The references to published works on other examples of the class of monuments described in this volume are much less complete than I could have wished; but they include all that I have been able to make available. The work is thus chiefly confined to descriptions of the actual results obtained by survey. Further comparisons with such works and deductions resulting therefrom must be left to those who may possess better means of reference.

BANGALORE, A. REA.
29th November 1892.

CONTENTS.

APPENDIX.

LIST OF PLATES.

REPORT

OF

THE ARCHÆOLOGICAL SURVEY OF SOUTHERN INDIA.

SOUTH INDIAN BUDDHIST ANTIQUITIES.

CHAPTER I.

CONSTRUCTION OF DOMES OF SOUTH INDIAN STÛPAS.

The evolution of the various forms of plan or construction which is seen in stûpas, would seem to have followed a definite course; and a consideration of it may form one of the indications which point to their relative dates. At first the stûpas were built solid; but when larger ones were undertaken, this was too laborious or expensive. The building of a hollow dome and filling it with earth might be satisfactory in a small structure; but in a large one, it would not be a success, for the walls would fracture and fall out. Various expedients, such as the construction of masonry floors across the earth-packing, would be tried; and latterly the idea of placing interior supporting walls would suggest itself.

In describing the results of the excavations recently conducted at the three stûpas of Bhaṭṭiprôḷu, Guḍivâḍa and Ghaṇṭasâlâ, it may be of interest to compare the different methods employed in the construction of the brick domes of these, with those of the other South Indian stûpas as yet examined. These buildings are ten in number, and are all situated in the Kṛishṇa district.[1] Some others there are at Nâgalapalle in the Ellore taluk of the Godávari district, but they are simply very small dâgobas grouped on platforms and are built of stone; they are hollow domes filled with earth. Except these, no other stone-built examples are known in Madras. In the construction of immense hollow domes of semi-spherical or flatter section, having no trace of arching, but with unmortared bricks laid from base to summit in horizontal courses, even though—as is not always the case—the bricks were good, it is evident that to prevent fracture, especially at the crown, some considerable skill was required. When the dome was of solid brick, only the secureness of the foundation would require to be looked to; but in the majority of these examples, this construction, whether from the expense of the immense number of bricks necessary or otherwise, has not been adopted. The materials used for packing the centre are earth, mud and concrete. In small structures, where sinking of the foundations, and consequent fracture of the masonry is not liable to occur, an earthen packing may be perfectly safe; but in large domes, any sinking of the wall may cause cracks which admit moisture, when the

---

[1] Amarâvati, Bhaṭṭiprôḷu, Guḍivâḍa, Garikapâḍ, Jaggayyapêṭa, Pedda Maddûr, Pedda Gañjâm (three stûpas), and Ghaṇṭasâlâ.

expansion and contraction of the material is certain to cause the destruction of the dome. In some cases, this has been obviated by brick, concrete, or stone floors stretching across the interior at intervals in the height. Examples occur at Jaggayyapêṭa, Garikapâḍ, and Pedda Gañjâm. Others have cross walls in the interior with a mud-packing. Examples are at Ghaṇṭaśâlâ and Pedda Gañjâm. Solid domes are found at Guḍivâḍa and Bhaṭṭiprôḷu; and these are undoubtedly the earliest of these stûpas. Properly made concrete is as secure as masonry, and, where limestone is abundant, can be cheaply made. This consideration may have led to its use at the Garikapâḍ stûpa. A simple earth-packing seems to have been generally employed only in the smaller buildings. The largest have interior cross walls in addition, or are of solid construction throughout. In few of these examples does sufficient of the facing of the superstructure remain to attest with certainty its original form. Most of them are razed to the level of the surrounding basement, with only a few courses of the upper exterior wall remaining; and a low mound of debris or masonry inside it. In the smaller structures, it may be confidently asserted that the dome was the form of outline. In the largest the building may have been constructed as a dome or in storeys. Those about which there is any question are Amarâvati, Guḍivâḍa and Ghaṇṭaśâlâ. When Colonel Mackenzie first saw the Amarâvati stûpa, "the central or higher portion of the mound was still untouched, and rose in a turreted shape to a height of 20 feet, with a diameter of about 90 feet at the top, and had been cased round with bricks.[1] Its then form may, however, have been due to its being ruined; its original shape was probably a dome as represented on the sculptures. On account of the centre of the Amarâvati stûpa having been completely destroyed before accurate observations of its interior construction were made, it is now impossible to know whether it may have been constructed of solid brick or otherwise. Colonel Mackenzie, who visited the site in 1797, states:[2] "I found a circular trench about 10 feet wide, dug about 12 feet deep, into a mass of masonry, composed of bricks of 16 inches square and 4 inches thick. It is probable that this body of masonry did not extend to a greater depth. The central area was untouched; and a mass of rubbish was thrown outside of the ditch, which prevented any observation of its original state; but I conjecture that the whole had, previous to its opening, formed a solid circular mound." The base of this building was about 138 feet in diameter.[3]

The stûpa at Bhaṭṭiprôḷu has a dome 132 feet and a base 148 feet in diameter. It is solid brick throughout.[4] The bricks are of very superior manufacture. At Bhaṭṭiprôḷu, a portion of the facing wall of the dome remains at the south-east quadrant. It is 5 feet 6 inches in height and has a batter inwards of 1 foot 2 inches, thus showing that it was a dome of a section of less than a semi-diameter.

The Guḍivâḍa stûpa has been constructed of solid and well-made brick. It has been so much demolished that its size and form cannot now be ascertained; but, from what remains, it would seem to have approached those at Amarâvati and Bhaṭṭiprôḷu.

The Ghaṇṭaśâlâ stûpa is 122 feet 2 inches in diameter at the base and 111 feet at the wall above it. Its plan differs from any others known in the Madras Presidency. The nearest approach to it is the second stûpa at Pedda Gañjâm. It has an outer ring of brick-work 18 feet 3 inches thick, exclusive of the basement, which is 5 feet 7 inches broad. Inside is a concentric circle 65 feet 10 inches in exterior diameter, and with a wall 3 feet 6 inches thick: this seems to have been the dome wall. In the centre is a square cube of

---

[1] Burgess: *Amar. and Jagg. Stûpas*, p. 20.
[2] *Ibid.*, p. 13.
[3] *Ibid.*, p. 21.
[4] Madras G.O., No. 207 P., of 22nd April 1892.

solid brickwork surrounded by a hollow brick square. Cross and radiating walls connect these other walls; the small cells or chambers thus formed are firmly packed with black mud. The bricks of which the walls are constructed are of very inferior make. At Ghaṇṭaśâlâ, the interior walls would suggest storeys as having been employed. These walls may, of course, have been used simply to strengthen the outer wall if it rose in the form of a dome; but its thickness of 18 feet 3 inches is proportionately much greater for a dome wall than in any of the other examples, where a ring dome was undoubtedly employed. The wall of the inner circle is of the usual proportions, and the dome would seem to have risen over it.

The stûpa at Garikapâḍ is constructed of an outer brick ring, 8 feet thick at the base, with alternate layers of concrete and earth in the centre. Its diameter across the base is 81 feet.[1]

At Jaggayyapêṭa, the stûpa has an outer brick casing with an interior packing formed of "layers of earth about 2 feet thick, over each of which was laid a close flooring of very large bricks closely fitted together." The diameter of the building is 31½ feet.[2]

The remains of the small stûpa discovered on the hill at Pedda Maddûr near Amarâvati show a diameter of 44 feet 6 inches, with a base wall 4 feet thick. It seems to have been packed with earth laid over a mass of large boulders.[3]

The largest of the three stûpas at Pedda Gañjâm has been a hollow brick dome, packed with earth. A floor of packed stones runs across the interior near the foundations and may have been repeated at intervals in the height. In the centre of the foundations are a number of bricks in the form of a svastika. The diameter of the building at the base is 74 feet, with a wall thickness there of 10 feet. The dome wall has been 3 feet thick.[4]

In the remains of the second stûpa at Pedda Gañjâm, the plan is two concentric brick circles separated from each other by a breadth of 4 feet 10 inches, and the two connected by twelve cross walls radiating from the centre; four of these walls project inside the inner circle. The exterior diameter of the outer circle is 38 feet 10 inches, with a wall thickness of 3 feet 10 inches; the outer diameter of the inner circle is 21 feet 6 inches, with a wall of 2 feet. As only one course of the bricks remains, it is impossible to say what the packing has been, but it was probably earth.[5] The foundations of a third stûpa were found here, having a diameter of 32 feet. It is a brick ring packed with earth, having a square pit in the centre packed with stones. Whether these latter extended up to the crown is uncertain.

Every one of these buildings has or had a square projection on the basement at each of the cardinal points opposite the four entrance gateways in the rail. From sculptured representations, these seem to have been intended as an architectural feature to give prominence to, or support the five stelae, which stood opposite these points near the dome. In the earliest stûpas, such as Bhaṭṭiprôḷu, Jaggayyapêṭa, and Garikapâḍ, of the marble slabs which encased the basement, only those at the projections were sculptured.

It has been thought that the curious small circular shaft in the centre of the Bhaṭṭiprôḷu stûpa might have been the receptacle for the strong wooden post that supported the covering umbrellas. A similiar but square shaft was found in the centre of the Ghaṇṭaśâlâ stûpa. That building has a greater proportional height of the dome intact, and the top of this shaft was closed with original brickwork, so that with it—unless the well had been again resumed

---

[1] Madras G.O., No. 383 P., of 30th April 1889.

[2] Burgess: *Amar. and Jagg. Stûpas*, pp. 107, 108.

[3] Madras G.O., No. 383 P., of 30th April 1889.

[4] Madras G.O., No. 703 P., of 14th July 1888.

[5] *Ibid.*

at a greater height,—it could not have served the purpose supposed. It may also have been so with the Bhaṭṭiprôḷu stûpa, though now, of course, it is impossible to ascertain whether it really was so. There seems reason to believe, from the fact of a stone umbrella post found at Nâgalapalle, from the umbrellas being stone, and from the sculptured representations, that the umbrella post also was of the same material. The small well may have served as a receptacle for fixing a sweep during the progress of building to guide the correct laying of the circular rings of brickwork.

CHAPTER II.

RAILS.

The detached enclosing rail is a well-known feature of these buildings, but in the examples under note, no remains of any have been found except at Amarâvati and more recently at Bhaṭṭiprôḷu. The most complete rail is that at Amarâvati; its features have been fully described by Dr. Burgess. The subject generally has been treated by Mr. Fergusson.[1] His remarks refer chiefly to North Indian stûpas; the only one in the south, about which much was then known was Amarâvati. Most, if not all of these buildings in South India, have been greatly demolished, and we cannot expect to gather from their remains any very complete ideas of their construction, but much may be gained by a careful piecing together of what has been left of them. From an examination of these buildings, it seems doubtful if any detached rail ever did exist at some at least of the smaller ones. These stûpus generally have a flooring of bricks, or stone flags extending and forming a lower procession path around the basement, on the outer edge of which stood the principal rail, where one existed. Of the rail at Bhaṭṭiprôḷu, only a fragmentary portion has been uncovered. The size and spacing of the piers would seem to show that the cross-rails had been lenticular in shape and unsculptured like some fragments of one which were found at Amarâvati, and are now being pieced together and fitted up in the Madras Museum. It resembles one from Sâñchi, illustrated by Mr. Fergusson.[2]

Although every stûpa may not have had a detached rail, all would seem—to judge from examples which remain complete enough to show the feature—to have had an inner rail or parapet on the edge of the basement or raised procession path, formed by the casing slabs over-topping it, and a coping panel on the top of them. From sculptural representations Mr. Fergusson had inferred that this feature existed in the large tope at Sâñchi.[3] It is clearly shown on all the Chaitya slabs found at Amarâvati, and subsequently at Pedda Gañjâm and Ghaṇṭaśâlâ. Undoubted traces of this feature have been found at one of these stûpas. At Pedda Gañjâm a number of slabs, similar to plate XXVII of the present work, were found standing in position against the basement wall, with their tops above the floor line of the upper procession path. Traces of the brick support for the raised inner rail or balustrade over them also remained there. This must have consisted of a marble coping laid along the top of the casing slabs similar to some at Jaggayyapêṭa.[4]

At Ghaṇṭaśâlâ, the height of the basement wall against which casing slabs would, as usual, be placed is 4 feet 3 inches. The heights of two slabs which have been found (pls. XXVII and XXVIII) are 4 feet 9 inches and 4 feet 7½ inches. If these slabs were among those from the basement wall, and,—as such panels have only been found in this position—it seems probable that they were, it is evident that independent of any coping over them their tops would surmount the procession path. Examples of coping slabs which must have been so placed are elsewhere illustrated (pls. XVI and XXVI).

---

[1] *Ind. and East. Arch.*, p. 84 et. seq. [2] *Ibid.*, pl. 30. [3] *Ibid.*, p. 64.
[4] *Amar. and Jagg. Stûpas*, pls. LI, figs. 1 and 3, and LIV, fig. 2.

The preceding observations refer chiefly to the stûpas built of brick, which have the upper procession path, round the base of the dome, of a breadth about equal to or greater than the height of the surrounding basement wall. In this, their proportions differ considerably from some in the north. Sâñchi, for example, has a basement height of 14 feet, and an offset above it of about 6 feet.[1] The buildings at Nâgalapalle form an exception to the rule followed in the others. As has been remarked, however, they are mere small structural stone dâgobas. Their proportions are identical with a rock-cut dâgoba in an adjoining cave. One of the largest is 15 feet in diameter, with a base 7 feet in height, and an offset over it with a breadth of 12 inches only. This, it is evident, is only a simulation of the architectural feature of a procession path, though it could not have been used as such. It would require no balustrade or rail around it.

[1] Fergusson: *Ind. and East. Arch.*, p. 64.

DETAILS OF CONSTRUCTION OF THE STÛPA.

Fig. 1. Arrangement of bricks in the centre.

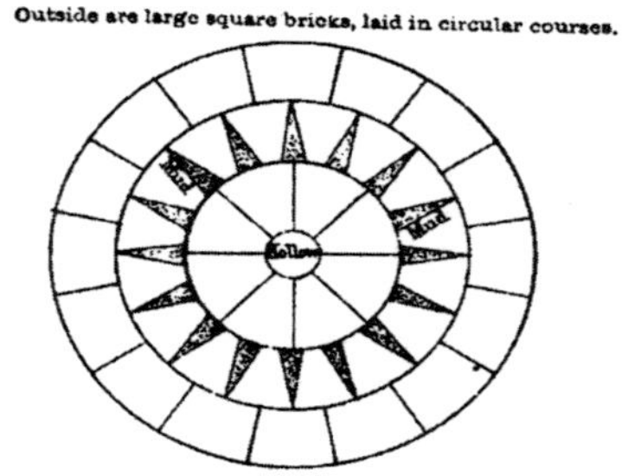

Fig. 2. Section of Central Excavated Well.

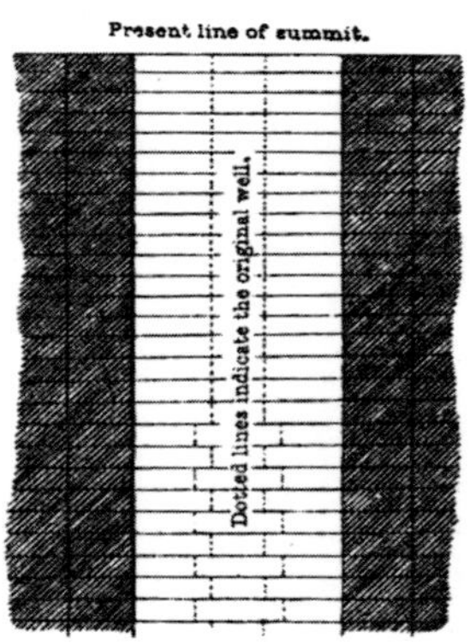

Fig. 3. Section of lower part of Dome, and raised procession-path at south-east quadrant.

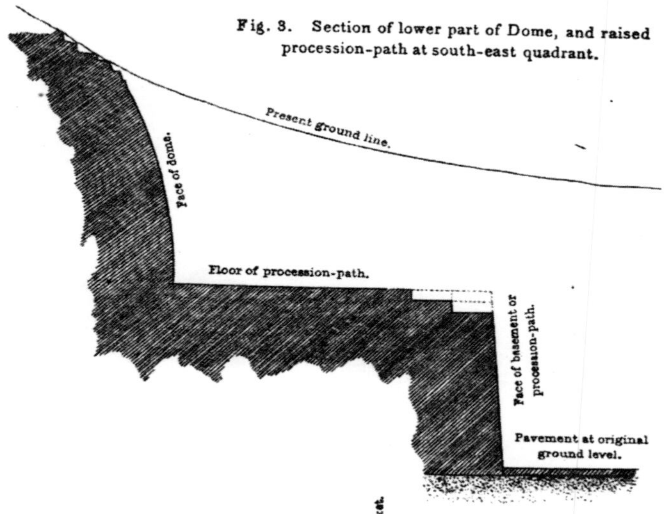

Fig. 4. Section of the lower part of a Marble Rail Pier.

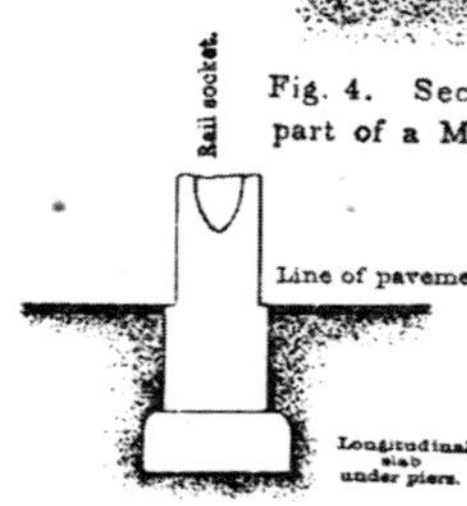

Fig. 5. Plan of Rail Piers, uncovered on north side.

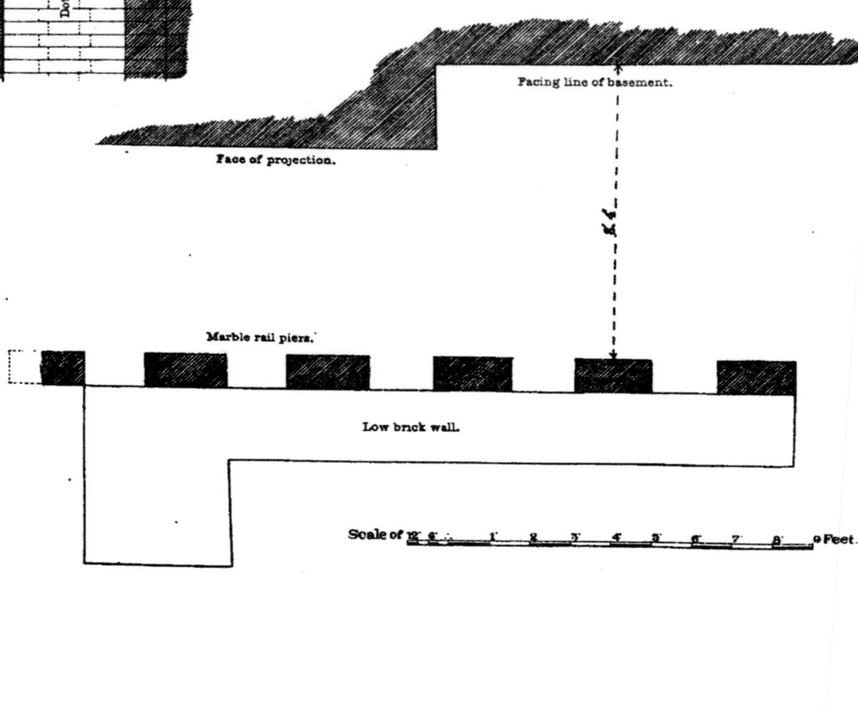

Litho., S. I. O., Calcutta

CHAPTER III.

BHAṬṬIPROḶU.—PREVIOUS EXPLORATIONS AT THE STÛPA.

A village in the Rêpalle taluk of the Kṛishṇa district, standing 4 miles from the right bank of the main channel of the Kṛishṇa river, and about 24 miles west by south from Masulipatam.

On the south of the village is a mound known as Lañja dibba, which covers the remains of a Buddhist stûpa. The mound is one of those mentioned in Mr. Boswell's report (1870). It was again referred to by Sir Walter Elliot, in a letter printed in Government Proceedings of 7th June 1871. In the same year, some correspondence took place regarding the destruction of the mound for the materials it contained. The bricks, being of large size and good quality, were used for road-making, and the marbles variously utilized in the construction of a sluice in the Kṛishṇa canal. Some of these may at present be seen built into the bed of the sluice. As a result of the attention thus called to it, the mound was afterwards inspected by Mr. Norris, Assistant Engineer, who submitted a report to the Madras Government.[1] A note was also published in the *Indian Antiquary*.[2] He found the mound to be a solid mass of brickwork of very irregular shape, owing to a great part of it having been demolished for road metal; but the form was evidently circular. It was constructed of bricks about 1′ 6″ × 2′ 0″. Its height was about 14 feet, and area about 1,700 square yards. On the top was a small circular hole, surrounded by eight bricks, which reached from top to bottom. An earthen bank, which existed around, had been formed by the dust and refuse remaining from the demolitions which had, from time to time, been made. The mound seemed originally to have been a cone, with side slopes of one horizontal to two vertical. He thus estimated the original height to have been about 66 feet.

Some years later the tope was visited by Mr. Sewell, whose report was printed by the Madras Government.[3] He elicited the following facts: " . . . . I must premise that " the tope is now absolutely demolished, and I could discern no trace of any sculptured stones " there. The village people told me that it had been a lofty mound up to a quite recent date, " though they varied a good deal as to its height. Previous to the demolition it had shown " the procession path round the top of the base of the dome, and they declared that it had " been surrounded by a marble railing or wall about 4 feet high. They said that this " wall had been partially standing at the time that the tope was destroyed and that the " slabs had been utilized, some by being burnt for lime, and others by being employed in " the construction of the Vellatur sluice. One of the employés of the Public Works Department " also told me that there had been a wall of Palnád marble, and that it had surrounded " the tope. He said that this marble wall was not sculptured, but that there had stood close " by a detached pillar about 15 feet high, which bore figures of men and animals. He however " differed from the villagers in saying that the marble had not been burnt for lime nor utilized " in any way on the road.

---

[1] Proceedings of the 11th October 1872.

[2] Vol. III, April 1874, p. 134.

[3] G.O., No. 1620, of 1st November 1878, pp. 33, 34.

"That there really were marble sculptures is tolerably conclusively proved by the fact "that in the walls and floor of this very Vellatúr sluice marbles have been extensively used. "Some sculptured stones bear carvings assimilating in type to those at Amarâvati though "they do not appear to have been so beautifully executed.

"There can be little doubt, therefore, that up to recent times this tope was the best pre-"served in the locality. It had the dome, probably not perfect, but at any rate in fair "preservation. It had at least one standing *Lát*. It had the procession path clearly apparent, "and it had a marble wall or railing round it. Mr. Norris has called attention to the curious "circular shaft, a few inches in diameter, running down the centre of the dome, which was "probably the receptacle for the strong wooden post that supported its covering umbrella or "umbrellas. All this has disappeared, and in its place remains a shapeless heap of earth "and broken brick, 14 feet high at its highest, while the canal water streams muddily over "the last fragmentary remains of marble rails and sculptured *Lát*. . . . ."

Mr. Sewell elsewhere remarks:[1] "I have it direct from the officer chiefly concerned "in the demolition that the mound was between 30 and 40 feet high, of a circular shape like a "dome, but ruined at the top; that there was a marble pillar standing erect, and sculpture here "and there in marble, but he does not remember rails or walls of marble. He found inside the "dome a casket made of six small slabs of stone dove-tailed into one another, measuring "about $2\frac{1}{2}' \times 1\frac{1}{2}' \times 1'$. Inside this was a common clay chatty, and inside the chatty a neat "casket made of soap-stone,[2] which contained a crystal phial. In the phial was a pearl, "a few bits of gold leaf and some ashes. Wishing to remove his discoveries, the stone casket "was accidentally broken and the remains were left at Bhaṭṭiprôḷu. The chatty was also "broken. The 'soap-stone' casket was smashed during a voyage to England and the frag-"ments thrown away. The crystal phial was presented to Dr. Burnell."

Mr. Boswell in a report[3] to the Madras Government, and referring to the remains at Bhaṭṭiprôḷu, says that during the demolition a stone casket was found, "inside of which "was a crystal vial with some seed, pearls, &c. The natives say that another bottle was broken "in digging, which contained the secret of alchemy, the substance capable of turning all other "metals to gold. They also firmly believe these structures cover some hidden treasure, and "from the fact of a five-headed Naga being discovered, this has been taken to fix the actual "amount at five crores . . . . These remarkable structures have been entirely covered "up and buried with a mass of earth, which has preserved them through long centuries, during "which their history and purposes have almost perished and have certainly become forgotten "in the neighbourhood, where they were originally raised. With all the interest that attaches "to the Buddhist era of Indian History, it becomes us to deal reverently with these relics "that time has spared. They are the evidences of a past age of civilization. When we have "carefully disinterred them and brought to light the symmetry and proportions of their "architectural designs, we shall probably find that they are worthy of a better fate than "to make district roads."

---

[1] *Topographical Lists of Antiq.*, vol. I, p. 77.

[2] "By 'soap-stone' I understand a material similar to that of which the Amarâvati casket at the Madras Museum is composed."

[3] Proceedings of 14th December 1871.

BHAṬṬIPRÔḶU.

PLATE III.

Inscribed Stone Relic Caskets.

Fig. 1.

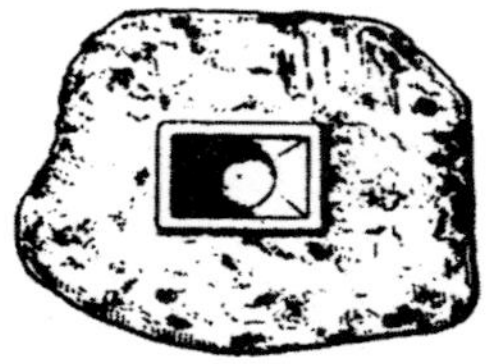

Fig. 2

No. 1. Casket.

Section of Receptacle of No. 1.

Section of Lid of No. 1.

Fig. 3.

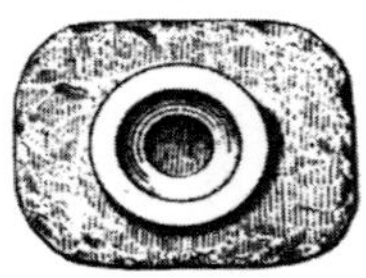

Fig. 4.

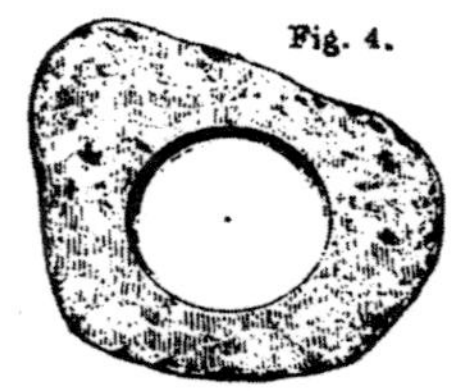

No. 2. Casket.

Section of Receptacle of No. 2.

Section of Lid of No. 2.

Fig. 5.

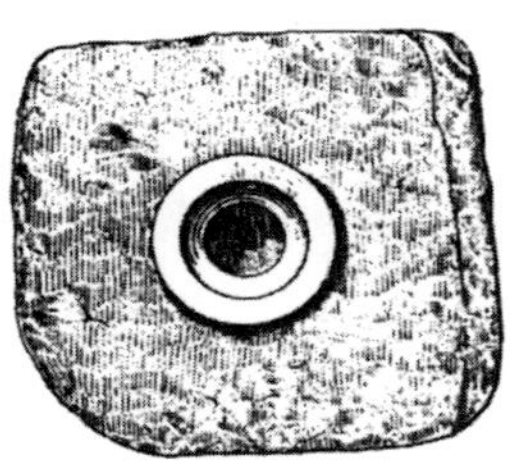

Fig. 6.

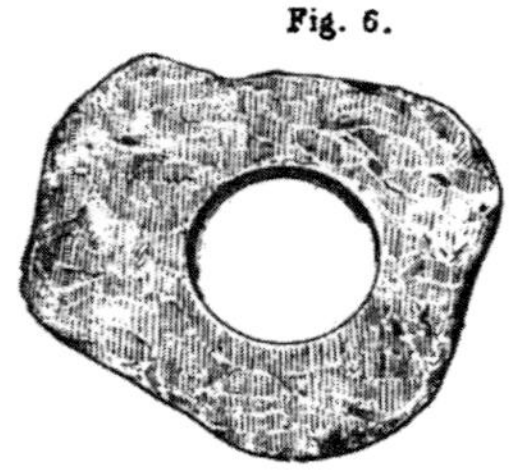

No. 3. Casket.

Section of Receptacle of No. 3.

Section of Lid of No. 3.

NOTE.—Inscriptions on the caskets are not shown.

Scale of 12 6 ... 1 2 3 Feet.

CHAPTER IV.

EXCAVATION IN THE CENTRE, WITH DISCOVERY OF CASKETS AND RELICS.

The foregoing extracts represent all the published information available regarding this building. As a result of my visit in the beginning of the present year (1892), I learned that the above-mentioned casket had been found at a point just above the present summit of the mound. But as the principal deposit is usually placed down in the centre near the foundations, or at the level of the raised procession path which surrounds these buildings, and as the summit of the mound is at present 15 feet above that level, I considered it very probable that other relics might yet exist, buried down in the centre of the solid brickwork. The mound is now of very irregular shape, the upper half of the dome and about a quarter of the mass of brickwork of the outer radius on the north-east and west sides having been removed. Solid brickwork, earth and loose bricks appear all over it. On tracing the circular courses of solid brick on the top of the mound, it is found that the real centre of the buildings is, on account of the demolition, not now in the middle of the mound, but considerably to the north of it. This spot was carefully concealed under a covering of loose bricks and earth, and required some search to find it. On the debris being removed, the central courses were found to be untouched, and exactly as described by Mr. Norris, with the addition, that, outside the eight large bricks which radiate around the small central well, there is another ring of sixteen wedge-shaped bricks each placed with the apex pointing to the centre. The triangular spaces between these bricks are filled in with clay. In the next course, the bricks are placed under the clay thus forming a sort of bond, and so on with each alternate course. The plan of any one course, thus, has a perhaps not unintended resemblance to a lotus flower. Outside extend the circular rings of ordinary rectangular-shaped bricks (pl. II, figs. 1 and 2). The small well in the centre was filled with earth; but, at the time the top of the stûpa was removed, it appears to have been open, and was then sounded for a depth of about 15 feet from the present surface. On removing the central ring of bricks, I found that the small central well went down with its sides straight for a depth of 5 feet 9 inches from the surface. Below that, the courses were stepped, leaving alternate diameters of 9½ inches and 1 foot 3 inches (fig. 2). Among the earth removed from the centre at the beginning of these steps was a small flat piece of black stone, a piece probably of the formerly found and broken casket. The excavation resulted in the unearthing of three inscribed votive caskets containing inner stone and crystal caskets, relics and jewels. They were placed at different levels near the foundations.

Plate I.

This plate shows the articles found during the excavation in the centre; it is divided by horizontal lines into three compartments. The uppermost shows the contents of the first receptacle. The articles in the upper part were those found surrounding the small globular stone casket. Those below them are the coins, beads, and flowers which were inside the globular casket. In the centre of the plate are the objects from the second casket. The lowest compartment has those from the third casket. Underneath stand the small inner caskets. On the left is the globular stone casket of the first receptacle with the cylindrical crystal phial, which stood inside it. In the centre is the second crystal phial. On the right is the third crystal phial and miniature beryl casket. These articles are now in the Madras Museum. They are described in detail in the following chapters.

CHAPTER V.

FIRST CASKET.

The bricks were removed for 14 feet 6 inches from the surface, or almost exactly on a level with the top of the raised basement or procession path which surrounds the dome, where a large irregular three-sided slab of black stone was found imbedded in the brickwork on the south side of the excavated shaft. It measures about 2′ 11″ × 2′ 6″. The two inner sides of the stone radiated from and touched the central well; its outer side was curved concentric with the brickwork. It proved to be the lid of a large stone relic casket (pl. III, fig. 2). Its under surface is smoothed, and has a rectangular cutting, measuring 11″ × 8″ × $\frac{1}{3}$″ deep. It lay on the top of another similar but thicker stone which formed the receptacle for a number of relics (fig. 1). Its size is 2′ 3″ × 1′ 10″ × 13″. On its upper surface is a cavity, 5 inches deep, and circular on the bottom, but sloping up to a rectangular top with raised rim made to fit into the hollow in the lid. The length of the rectangle lay east and west. The upper surface of the stone is smooth, and, cut on it around the casket chamber, are two lines of an inscription in a new type of the Southern Maurya character.[1] In the cavity stood a globular black stone relic casket (pl. IV, fig. 7). Around this casket and mixed with the earth which filled the cavity were the following articles, of which a few are illustrated on the above plate: A copper ring (fig. 1), and several bits of copper; a small bead and two double pearls; two small semi-spherical cups made of a hard brown metal. They fit into each other, and are evidently the lid and receptacle of one vessel. On the apex of the lid is a gold bead. The other also has had a gold bead, which was found in the earth alongside (fig. 5). One bears traces of some sort of resin having been inside.

A hexagonal crystal (fig. 4, and pl. V [2]), with slightly convex sides, pierced with a hole through its axis. On each of the sides is lightly traced or scratched with one stroke for each line of the letters an inscription in a similar character to that on the stone. The first line of the inscription is indicated by a line drawn from the centre of the end to one of the angles. A similar but bent line appears on the other end in the middle of the third line of letters. It will be obvious that, being pierced, it must have been used for suspending around the neck, most probably as an amulet. Phylacterions were used by the Greeks and other nations of antiquity, and like this they usually bore inscriptions. The **Liṅgayats**, at the present day, suspend a like object, being a liṅga enclosed in a box.

Made of thin sheets of pure gold were two **triśulas** (pl. IV, figs. 2 and 3), and four flowers with eight petals, one of which is shown in figure 6. There were also a hollow single and a double gold bead and seven small triangular pieces of the same metal; these last are evidently pieces of a flower. As to the position these objects occupied in the cavity around the globular stone casket, the two small semi-spherical vessels lay on the west,

---

[1] For a note on this and the other inscriptions, see letter by Dr. Bühler in the *Academy* of 28th May 1892, *Jour. R. As. Soc.*, part 3, July 1892, pp. 602–609, and *Wiener Zeitschrift für die Kunde des Morgenlandes No.* 2, 1892. Translations will afterwards be published in the *Epigraphia Indica*.

[2] In the photographs in this plate two faces are shown on each figure. It was found that the reflection from the sides obliterated all trace of the letters when viewed in the camera. The remaining four sides of the prism had thus to be washed with indian ink. The two sides in the view were touched with chinese white, and this colour, being afterwards scraped off, left every letter, dot, or flaw on the two surfaces clear on the photograph.

the crystal prism, gold flowers, &c., on the east. The globular casket is $4\frac{1}{2}$ inches in diameter and height (fig. 7). The lid fits loosely on a groove in the lower portion. The inner cavity is cylindrical, and inside it stood a cylindrical crystal phial $2\frac{1}{2}$ inches in diameter by $1\frac{1}{4}$ inches in height (figs. 11 and 12). Its position in the globular stone casket is shown on figure 7. It is moulded on the sides, flat on the top and bottom and has its lid fitted in the same manner as the small receptacle which encloses it. Inside is a flat piece of bone, $\frac{1}{3}$ inch broad; it is smooth on the one side and celled on the other; its position in the crystal casket is shown on figure 12. The method of preserving the relic with the triple casket has perfectly served its purpose, for, though there were dust and earth in the two stone caskets, there was scarcely a speck in the crystal one. Inside the globular stone casket and lying below the crystal phial were nine small flowers of various sizes in gold leaf; one of the largest is shown on figure 8. Six hollow gold beads over $\frac{1}{8}$ inch in diameter (fig. 9), and eight smaller. Four small flowers in thin copper, similar to those in gold. Nineteen small pierced pearls, and a slightly blue coloured amethyst bead (fig. 10). Fixed on the bottom by oxidation and arranged in the form of a svastika (fig. 13) were twenty-four small silver coins. They are plain on the reverse; and on the obverse have Śrî-pâḍas, triśulas, lotus flowers, and other emblems more or less legible. In the svastika, nine coins were in the centre rectangle, three on each of the four arms, and the other three (fig. 14) over the centre. The flowers and beads seem also to have been originally arranged symmetrically. An example of this symbolical use of the svastika was found in the centre of the largest of the stûpas at Pedda Gañjâm.

BHAṬṬIPRÔḶU.

PRINCIPAL RELICS FROM FIRST CASKET.

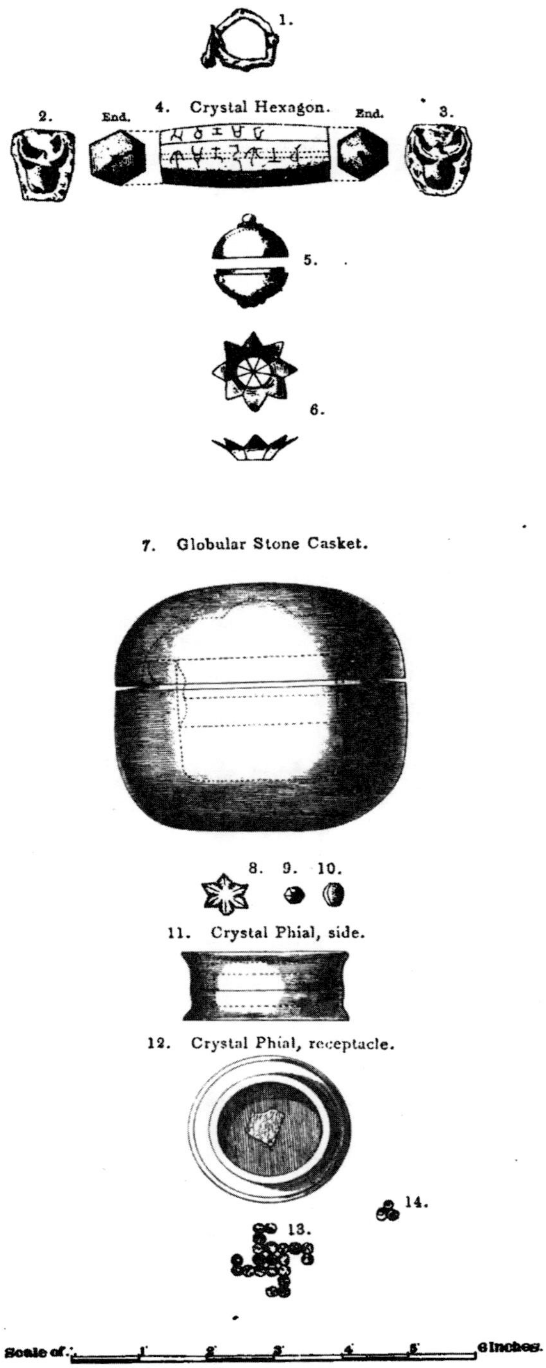

BHAṬṬIPRÔḶU. PLATE V.

THREE VIEWS OF INSCRIBED HEXAGONAL CRYSTAL, SHEWING THE SIX INSCRIBED FACES.

1.

2.

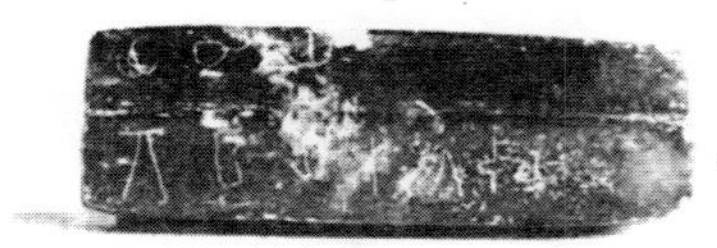

3.

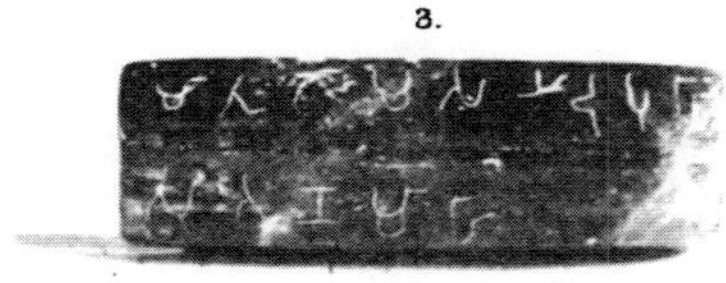

Photo-etching.

Survey of India Offices, Calcutta, December 1893.

CHAPTER VI.

SECOND CASKET.

The bricks in the shaft were removed for a further depth of 2 feet 6 inches below the level of the surface of the lid of the casket just described, or 17 feet in all from the top of the shaft, when another black stone was found on the north side of the well, and, like the first, sunk a foot into the side wall. It was the lid, and, another stone which lay below it, the receptacle of a second relic casket. The covering stone (pl. III, fig. 4) is roughly triangular in form with rounded corners, and measures about 2′ 3″ × 2′ × 10″. On the top is a circle 7½ inches in diameter, raised ¼ inch above the surface. The under side is smooth and has a circular space ½ inch deep and 12 inches in diameter. In this circle is an inscription in 19 lines, while around it is another in two lines: the letters were all filled in with white. The stone receptacle (fig. 3) is roughly rectangular, with rounded corners, and measures 1′ 8″ × 1′ 4″ × 12″. On its upper surface is a circular hole 6¼ inches deep, 7½ inches in diameter at the top and 4 inches at the bottom. Around the top is a raised rim, 1½ inches broad, which fits into the hollow in the lid. Around and outside the rim is an inscription in two lines. These letters also are filled in with white. The cavity was nearly filled with earth, and had no inner stone casket as with the first. In it was a crystal phial (pl. VI, fig. 1) 1⅝ inches in diameter by 2¾ inches high. Its lid is moulded like a dâgoba. The hollow in the vessel is cylindrical. The top and bottom were lying separate and filled with earth. There was no sign of a relic inside. The following articles were found among the earth in the stone cavity:—164 gold flowers of varying sizes such as are illustrated in figures 2 to 6; some are plain and others have dots around the petals; they have six, eight and nine petals, and some have been fitted inside each other with a gold bead as a bud (fig. 11). Two circular flowers (figs. 7 and 8); a two-armed figure (fig. 9), and two trinacrias (figs. 10 and 12). All these are in gold leaf or thin sheets of gold. Two gold stems for flowers, one of them attached (fig. 14). Six hollow gold beads (fig. 15), and a small coiled gold ring (fig. 13). Two pearls, a garnet, six coral beads (figs. 19, 20 and 21), and a bit of the same material. A slightly blue flat oval crystal bead and a pointed oval white crystal bead (fig. 17). Two flat six-sided chrysolite or beryl drops (figs. 16 and 18). There were a number of bits of corroded copper leaf, including flowers, stems, and a miniature umbrella. The remains of a small silver Śasanam. The metal of this is very thin, almost completely corroded, and in consequence extremely brittle, so that it seems uncertain whether it will be possible to unfold it. It has been a long strip of metal 1⅝ inches broad, wound in a roll to about eight thicknesses and pressed flat (fig. 22). Three lines of letters have been pricked on the side folded inwards. The largest piece is 2 inches in length. At first, it was covered with green corrosion, doubtless due to its lying among the pieces of copper; but on a partial cleaning, the white metal appeared.

CHAPTER VII.

THIRD CASKET.

At a depth of 18 feet from the surface, the third and last casket was found lying on the east side of the shaft. The lid is an irregular circular stone measuring about 2 feet 3 inches across by from 9 to 10 inches thick (pl. III, fig. 6). On its under surface is a circular space sunk $\frac{1}{2}$ inch, having an inscription in eight lines, with letters whitened. The stone receptacle which it covered is roughly square in shape, and measures 2′ 5″ × 2′ 3″ × 11″ (fig. 5). On the upper surface is a circular cavity $5\frac{3}{4}$ inches deep, $7\frac{1}{2}$ inches in its upper diameter, and 5 inches at the bottom. Around it is a rim $2\frac{1}{4}$ inches broad, which fits into the hollow in the lid. Outside the rim is a circular inscription in one line, with letters whitened. The cavity was nearly filled with earth. In it were a crystal phial of the shape of that found in the second casket, but slightly larger (pl. VI, fig. 23). The hollow in this vessel is cup-shaped. The phial is $2\frac{1}{8}$ inches in diameter by 3 inches high. The two pieces lay apart and were filled with earth. Close to the phial lay a miniature relic casket made of a beryl (figs. 24, 25 and 26). Thus, as with the first casket, this had a triple receptacle, and owing to this the relics were found intact in the innermost one. They are three small pieces of bone. The beryl casket had originally stood inside the phial, as shown in figure 23. A cylindrical hole, $\frac{3}{32}$ inch in diameter, is drilled in its axis, in which are the relics. The hole is closed by a small white crystal stopper with hexagonal top, with a sheet of gold leaf fixed on to it. A loose sheet of the same material closes the joint at the necking, and another is placed outside on the bottom. The total height of the casket is ·75 inch.

Two amethyst beads (figs. 30 and 31) and a yellow crystal bead. A small hexagonal crystal drop of a slightly yellow colour (fig. 32), and another flat one of white crystal (fig. 29), a bone bead (fig. 33).

Six pearls and thirty-two seed pearls, all pierced. Thirty flowers, similar to those above described, a bent two-armed figure (fig. 27), and a quatre-foil (fig. 28), all in gold leaf. A piece of what appears to be silicate; an apparently iron cinder; and a few bits of copper.

The bricks were removed from the shaft, down to the foundations, which were found to be 23 feet from the summit of the mound. The brickwork in the centre is thus 3 feet below the level of the brick flooring which surrounds the stûpa.

BHAṬṬIPRÔḶU.

PLATE VI.

INSCRIBED STONE RELIC CASKETS.

Fig. 1.

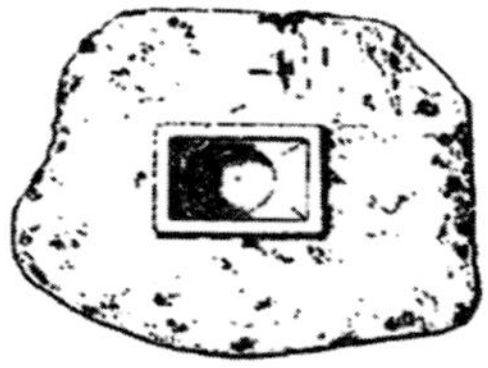

Fig. 2

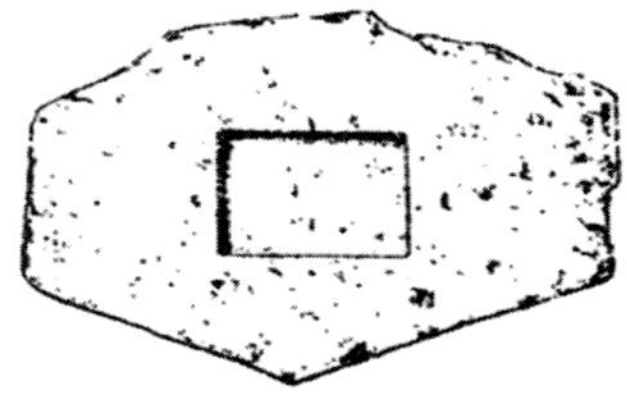

No. 1. Casket.

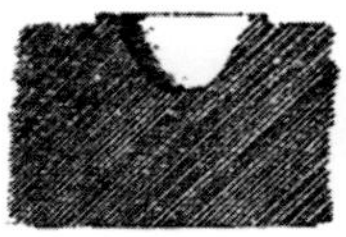

Section of Receptacle of No. 1.

Section c

Fig. 3.

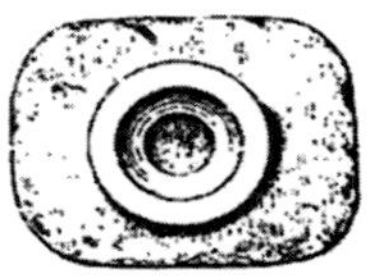

Fig. 4.

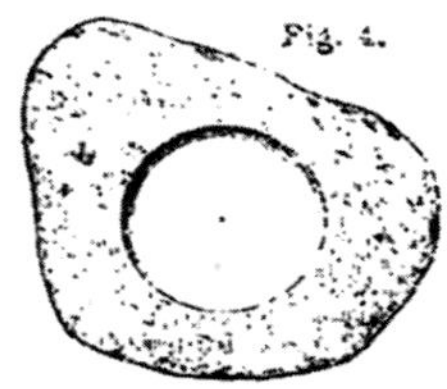

No. 2. Casket.

Section of Receptacle of No. 2.

Section of Lid of No. 2.

Fig. 5.

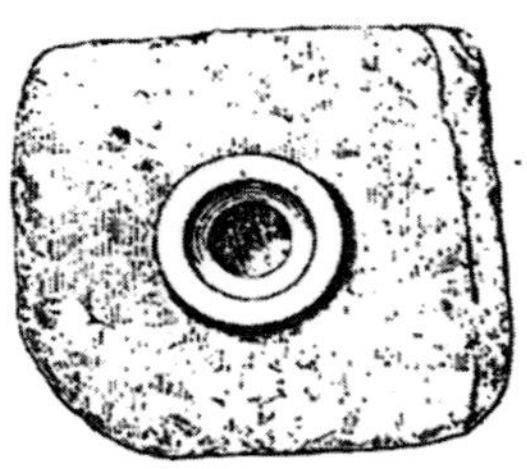

Fig. 6.

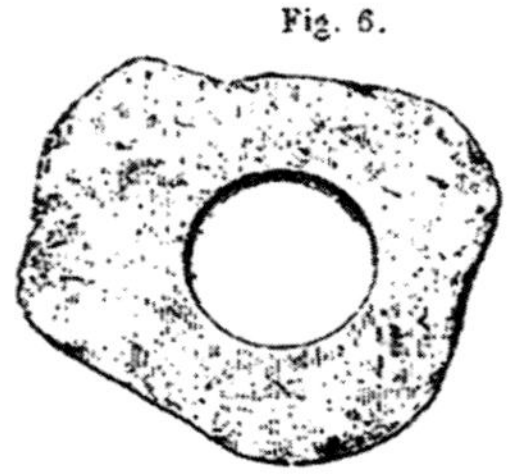

No. 3. Casket.

Section of Receptacle of No. 3.

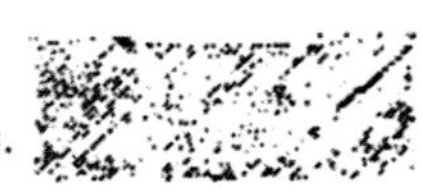

Section of Lid of No. 3.

NOTE.—Inscriptions on the caskets are not shown.

Scale of 12" 6" 1 2 3 Feet

CHAPTER VIII.

EXCAVATION AROUND THE BUILDING.

To ascertain what size the building had been, and whether any marbles yet remained, some trenches were dug at points around the exterior of the brickwork. The brick basement, or raised procession-path at the south-east quadrant, was found unbroken; but no marble slabs remain against it. The unbroken face of the dome also, at this point, remains intact for a height of over 5 feet above it. A section is shown on plate II, figure 3. The radius, from the centre of the building to this remaining portion of the wall of the dome, is 66 feet, making its diameter 132 feet; and, as the breadth of the surrounding basement is 8 feet, its diameter is thus 148 feet. For comparison as to size, it may be mentioned, that the base of the Amarâvati stûpa was about 138 feet in diameter.[1] Outside the raised basement, and eight feet below the surface, is a brick floor, on the outer edge of which, would once stand the marble rail, but the only remains of it were some traces of brickwork and chips of marble.

At the position of the north-east quadrant, the brick flooring between the basement and the rail remains. The basement itself has been removed, and a considerable portion of the brickwork of the dome inside the line of it. The mound which covers the remains of the central building is surrounded by another ring of mound on every side except the east. This outer ring is the earth thrown up during some of the previous excavations. On the north side, two parallel trenches were carried outwards from the position of the basement through this outer bank. These trenches were then connected by a cross cut. At this point some courses of the basement and of the north projection remain in position. I found here two pieces of a marble umbrella having a curve with a radius of 1 foot 6 inches (pl. VII, figs. 1 and 2); a small piece of a pilaster base from a slab (fig. 3); a pilaster capital with horses and riders (pl. VIII), and the half of what has been a large slab carved with the lower portion of a draped figure (pl. IX). The figure panel is checked on one side with a pilaster up its edge; and the portion of the drapery that remains, is but slightly raised from the surface. The carving is in the same archaic style as in those from the stûpas at Jaggayyapêṭa and Garikapâḍ. At a distance of 8 feet 4 inches from the basement, I found the remains of six marble bases of the rail standing in position (pl. II, fig. 5). They measure 1 foot 11 inches by 12 inches, by 1 foot 10 inches in height, above ground; with a space between each of 1 foot 7 inches. Some of them have a portion of the lower disc-shaped socket hole for the rail panel. They are sunk 1 foot 6 inches below the brick floor; and rest on a broad slab of marble laid longitudinally below them (fig. 4). Outside is a low brick wall. The ground was opened up for a few feet around these, but none others were seen there, nor any of the large panels which would surmount the rail. Similar trenches were dug on the west side, but though some courses of the basement remain, and several small plain slabs, splayed on one edge, were found outside it, no trace of the rail appeared. On the south, digging could not be carried out, on account of the proximity of a tank. Two octagonal piers, and a block of marble lie on the position of the north-east quadrant of the rail. The two former are illustrated on plate X, figures 1 and 2. Some small saucer-shaped earthenware

---

[1] Burgess: *Amar. and Jagg. Stûpas*, p. 21.

lamps, exactly similar to some found at Nâgalapalle, were dug out of the north trenches (pl. VII, figs. 4 and 5).

The space between the rail piers is about half that of Amarâvati, and I think the panels can hardly have been carved like those from that stûpa. They have probably been of plain lenticular shape, like those at Sâñchi. It is difficult to believe that all the large top-panels,—which would be sculptured—have gone: some must surely be lying under the earth bank outside the position of the rail.

That the basement wall panels, and not those of the rail, were the marbles removed and broken up for use on the canal, seems certain. An old maistri, and others who removed these stones, stated that the slabs were plain and about 4 feet square, standing with their tops about a yard underground. They had been removed from all around the wall. On seeing the portion of the south-east basement uncovered, the men recognized it as the position these slabs had occupied. These particulars agree with the depth of the basement underground, and the size of the slab now found. The portion of the rail, also, uncovered, shows that such slabs could not have been used in its construction. Everything would seem to point to a similarity of design and arrangement of the basement wall panels of this stûpa, and those at the two places named. Thus only the panels at the four cardinal projections of the basement would be sculptured. The line of slabs which surrounded, and which were removed from the face of the basement, would be plain, with the exception of a pilaster up one edge of each.

BHAṬṬIPRÔḶU.

Fig. 1.

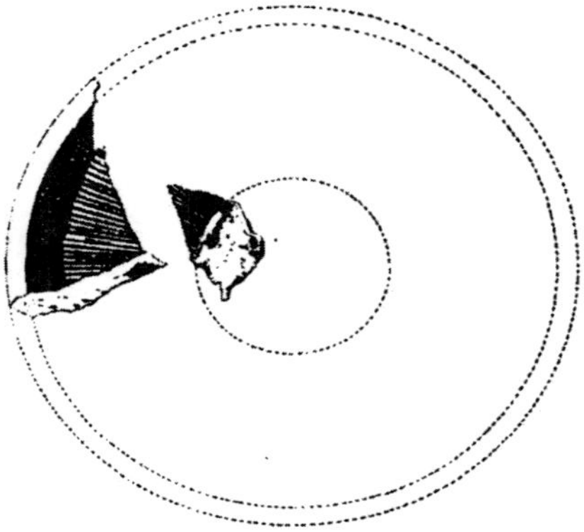

Fig. 2.

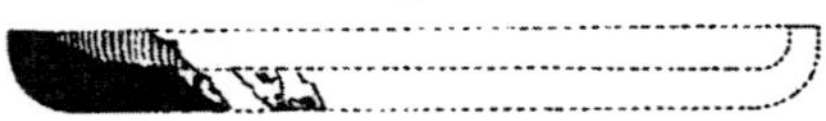

Scale of 12″ 9″ 6″ 3″ 1′ 2 Feet.

Scale for Figs. 1 and 2.

Fig. 3.

Scale of 12″ 9″ 6″ 3″ 1 Foot.

Scale for Fig. 3.

Fig. 4.

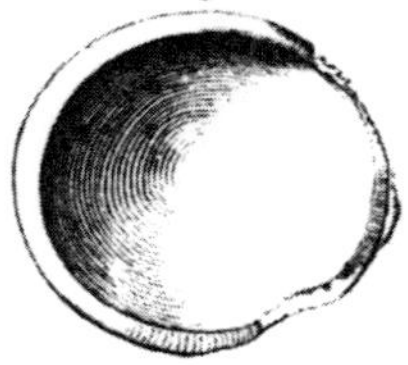

Fig. 5.

Scale of 1″ 2″ 3 Inches.

Scale for Figs. 4 and 5.

Photo., S. I. O., Calcutta.

BHAṬṬIPRÔḶU. PLATE VIII.

MARBLE CAPITAL OF THE PILASTER OF A CASING SLAB.

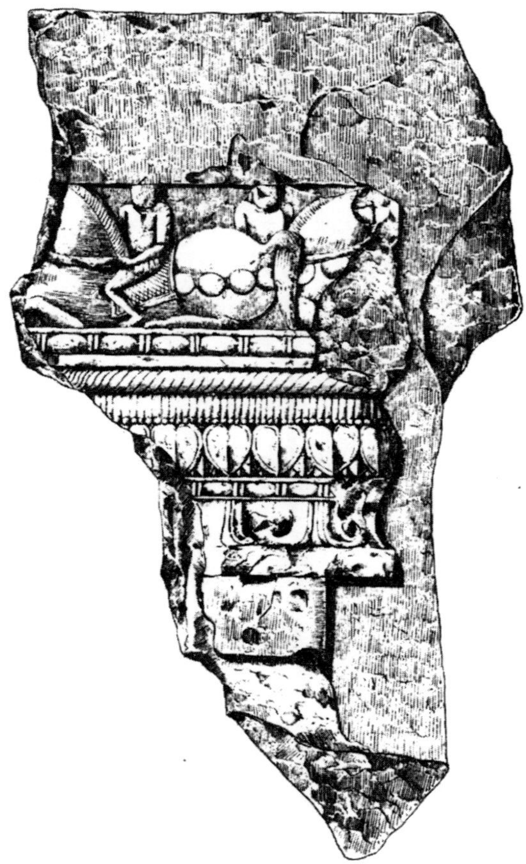

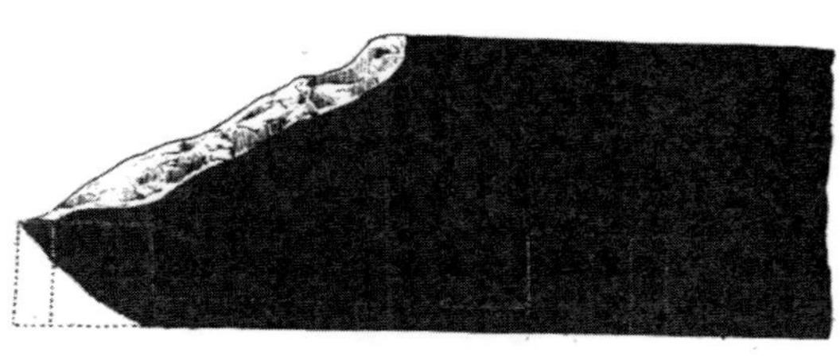

Scale of 12" 9" 6" 3" 1 Ft.

Litho., S. I. O., Calcutta.

BHAṬṬIPRÔḶU.

Lower Portion of Slab from North Projection of Basement.

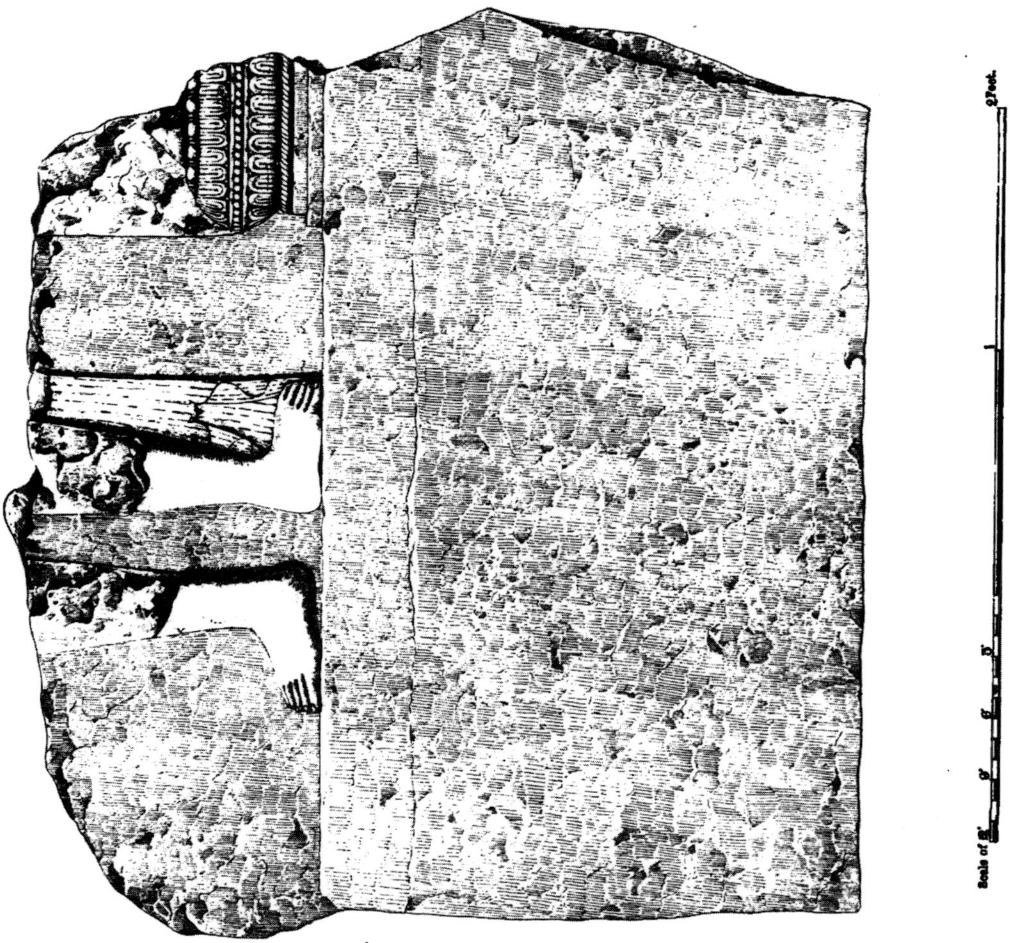

Thickness 3". Thickness 5".

Photo., S. I. O., Calcutta.

BHAṬṬIPRÔḶU.

MARBLE PIERS.

Fig. 1.

Plan.

Fig. 2.

Plan.

Scale of 12" 6" 1' 2' 3' 4' 5 6' 7' 8' 9' 10' 11 Feet.

CHAPTER IX.

REMAINS NEAR BHAṬṬIPRÔḶU. CHINNA-LAÑJA DIBBA.

Immediately on the east of the stûpa is the camping tope. It is a slightly-raised piece of ground known as Chinna-Lañja dibba. From the name, and the presence of bricks in the soil, it has probably been the site of a Buddhist building. A legend is current to the effect that a dancing girl had her residence here; the large mound was the temple where she worshipped. There is also a story of a "treasure" having been found many years ago at some spot in it, and a stone box or casket, similar to those recently taken from the centre of the large stûpa.

VIKRAMÂRKA KÔṬA DIBBÁ.

On the east outskirts of the village is a piece of ground under cultivation, and planted with mimosa trees. It is known by the above name, and is said to have been the site of the fort of the king who ruled here. A long low mound—one of the walls of the fort—can be traced for some distance. It is said that large bricks were found, while it was being dug into some "thirty years ago."

CHAPTER X.

THE STÛPA AT GUḌIVÂḌA.

This town is the taluk head-quarters, and stands twenty miles north-west of Masulipatam. The remains of the demolished Buddhist stûpa stand in a low mound in the village. The ground measures about 140 feet square. On the west and south are roads, and on the two other sides, house yards enclosed by mud walls, built on the slope of the mound. The mound is very much smaller than the one at Amarâvati, the slope of which extends for a very considerable distance beyond the outside limits of the building.

The existence of a stûpa at this place, was first brought to notice by Mr. Boswell in a report to the Government of Madras in 1870.[1] He states that "at Guḍivâḍa there is a circular mound resembling the one at Amarâvati. It is known as *lanja dibba* or harlot's mound. It is reported to have been raised by a dancing girl who lived on the top, and confined herself to one meal a day, of which she delayed to partake till she could see the lights of Akarepally Pagoda. The mound, however, evidently covers the ruins of a Buddhist dagoba. Well burnt bricks are found in large quantities. As there is no stone available in this neighbourhood, sculptures probably do not exist, but the people tell of a stone-casket dug up here containing a pearl, some gold leaf, and other relics. There are said to have been formerly ninety-nine Buddhist or Jain temples here and ninety-nine tanks." In a subsequent report,[2] Mr. Boswell makes reference to the stûpa having been excavated to provide bricks for road-making. In the orders by Government on the two above-quoted reports, instructions were issued for the protection of this and other Buddhist monuments in the district.

The locality was afterwards visited by Mr. Sewell, who concluded, from the appearance of the mound, that it was a brick-made tope of about the same dimensions as that at Sâñchi.[3] No trace could be found of any sculptures or rails as at Sâñchi and Amarâvati.

Mr. Sewell considered it possible that, in the absence of stone, the rail might have been made of brick or wood, and in consequence have been completely destroyed. It seems more probable, however, that, if a rail really existed, it would, as has been the case in every instance of the discovery of traces of one in a South Indian stûpa, be constructed of marble. In the majority of stûpas, some trace of marble construction has been found, though the material does not exist in the locality, and must have been conveyed for long distances, probably from the Palnâd, where the stone exists.[4] Dr. Burgess found, that the stone used in the Jaggayyapêṭa stûpa had been quarried on the bank of the Krishṇa, immediately to the south of that place; and that the same stone must have been used at Amarâvati.[5]

Mr. Sewell obtained from a subordinate of the Public Works Department the following description of the discoveries made in the mound when in progress of demolition. He states that "four stone receptacles were found at the four corners, each measuring about two feet by one foot six inches, formed by the erection, on one stone as a base, of four stones placed on their edge, with a covering slab. Inside each was a casket, but I could not

---

[1] G.O., No. 1725, of 7th November 1870.
[2] G.O., No. 2108, of 14th December 1871.
[3] Report in G.O., No. 1620, of 1st November 1878, p. 32.
[4] *Kistna District Manual*, p. 151.
[5] *Amar. and Jagg. Stûpas*, p. 107.

ascertain what material they consisted of, nor what they contained, nor can I ascertain what has become of them." In a letter from Sir Walter Elliot, published by the Madras Government,[1] the following reference occurs: About 1840, a mound of brickwork was demolished to obtain material for repairing the high road between Bezvâḍa and Bandar, and in it were found "four stone-vases, each containing a crystal reliquary, not deposited in the centre of the mound as at Dipal-dinna (Amarâvati) but in the four sides." . . . . "A similar deposit was found some years ago by the Zemindar of Pittapoor in the Rajahmundry district. The four stone-vases, each containing a crystal box, were seen by Sir Henry Montgomery in 1843, who induced the Rajah to send them to the Government Museum, where they now are. They were figured in the *Madras Journal of Literature and Science*, Vol. XV, and plate 2, but without any description, *Madras Journal*, Vol. XIX, p. 225." These stone boxes have since been figured and described by Dr. Burgess.[2] Four small crystal caskets, which seem to be those above referred to, have just (1892) been found in the Madras Museum. They are similar in shape, but smaller than the first crystal casket from Bhaṭṭiprôḷu. A slight difference is seen in their each having a small knob in the centre of the top of the lid. The description of the construction of the Guḍivâḍa caskets tallies with that of the casket found in the upper part of the Bhaṭṭiprôḷu stûpa, when it was being demolished: it also was made up of stone slabs. In the notes of the finding of these four caskets, it is uncertain which "four corners" are referred to, for it must be remembered the building is a circular one. The account does not state whether around or near the centre, or the circumference. They may have occupied positions similar to the lower ones at Bhaṭṭiprôḷu. From enquiries on the spot, one at least appears to have been found high up in the centre of the brick mound.

Though all traces of marble sculptures, or rail, had been removed from the surface, it was possible that some of them might remain underground, as at Amarâvti and elsewhere. This could only be ascertained by digging. Owing to the confined nature of the ground, there was very little room for trenches, and no digging could be done outside the limits of the mound; but at different points, on the west, north, and east sides, I had three trenches sunk on the boundaries of the ground. These showed that the foundations were three feet below the level of the roads; and the brickwork remained for a height of from nine to eleven feet at the highest parts. The walls stand close up to the boundaries, but as the faces are rough, it is impossible to ascertain how much further out the unbroken walls may have extended. The exact size of the stûpa cannot thus be known. Traces of circular courses of brickwork appear on the mound, and a very slight scraping of the earth, which has accumulated over it, shows that it is solid up to the centre. In this respect, its construction has been similar to that at Bhaṭṭiprôḷu.

---

[1] Proceedings of 7th June 1871, No. 1000.

[2] *Amar. and Jagg. Stûpas*, p. 99, pl. LIII.

CHAPTER XI.

SITE OF THE ANCIENT VILLAGE.

On the west outskirts of the town, the ground slopes upwards to an extensive mound now under cultivation. It is known as Lâmapâḍu dibba, and is the site of the fort, which enclosed the ancient village, with its traditionary ninety-nine Buddhist temples and tanks. Long low ridges of earth, each about a quarter of a mile in length, can be indistinctly traced; these form a large square, and mark the position of the walls of the fort. It is said to have been a place of importance in the transport of grain between Bezvâḍa and Ellûr.

Bricks and broken pottery are scattered about the ground; and small articles of interest are found when the earth is turned up, or after rain. The soil is composed of mud, the washed-down material of which the houses were built; it is largely used for brick-making. Regarding the objects found here, Mr. Sewell states,[1] "I have found there a large number "of coins, beads, and other small articles. A few of the coins have proved valuable. General "Cunningham, to whom I sent them, has made out the inscriptions on three of them, and "finds them to be coins of the Andhra kings *Gôtamiputra*, *Yâdnya Srî*, and *Srî Chanda.* "They bear well known Andhra dynasty devices. Another very interesting coin (I was in "possession of three, struck from different dies, but of the same design) bore the figure of "a Roman or Greek galley, with a rather crescent-shaped hull, two masts, and a large "oar-shaped rudder. All of the coins found were made of lead, and most of them were so des- "troyed as to have their devices quite undecipherable. I found also, very well preserved, the "terra-cotta head of a female, with braided hair caught up in a knot at the back, and fastened "round, apparently, with an ornamental metal band. The beads are made of hardened mud, "burnt clay, bone, crystal, glass, amber, and stones of various sorts including many garnets. "The beads are of very varied shapes and sizes, and many of them are of beautiful workman- "ship, notably those in stone. I found also several other small articles amongst the gravel, a "small portion of a crystal jar, one or two pieces of broken bone armlets, one or two small "polished stones, apparently fragments of burnishers, and other such like remains;—the whole "proving conclusively that the men of that day were highly experienced lapidaries. As to "the pottery, some of the broken fragments show that it was of a class vastly superior to that "of the present day—a fact which I apprehend there is little or no dispute about. The mouths "of some of the pots must have been three or four feet in diameter, and the pots themselves "must have been of very large size, and probably used for grain receptacles. Some are grace- "fully ornamented."

In the courtyard of the temple of Bhîmêśvara is a fine Jaina image (pl. XI). It is now claimed by the Brahmans, and worshipped as Munêśvarasvâmi. The figure is a seated one, and is carved on a black stone slab. The ear lobes are pierced and distended. The hair is curled. Over the head is a seven-headed nâga, and a triple umbrella. In plate XXXV is illustrated a curious monolithic sculptured Jaina column, lately unearthed by some excavators from under the foundations of a house at Bezvâḍa.

---

[1] *Report, ibid.*, p. 33.

GUḌIVÂḌA.

JAINA IMAGE.

Scale of 12' 9' 6' 3' 1 2 Feet.

Photo., S. I. O. Calcutta.

CHAPTER XII.

ANDHRA COINS FROM GUḌIVÂḌA

PLATES XII AND XIII.

These coins were found scattered in the earth on the site of the ancient village. They are seventy-two in number, and represent the best of a lot of one hundred and twenty which I secured during my visit. The whole of them are lead, and were all at first more or less covered with oxidation. Some of them, especially the smaller ones, at first appeared quite devoid of either device or inscription, so thick was the oxidised coating; but after being cleaned, these were generally found to have the most perfect devices preserved underneath. It will be apparent, therefore, that none of this kind of coin should be passed over as worthless, till an attempt has been made at cleaning. With a soft material like lead, some care is required in removing the deposit, so that the letters or emblems on the coin may not be injured. With some coins, the oxidation is so obstinate, that it is impossible to completely remove it, but in most cases it can be entirely taken off, or sufficiently so, to show what is underneath. Potash dissolves the salts of lead, and, I found, that soaking the coins in a solution of this material for a fortnight or three weeks, made it sufficiently soft to be easily rubbed off. During this period, the coins were regularly scraped with a quill, and, with what I afterwards found to be more effective, a stalk of the *calotropis gigantea* (எருக்கும்செடி-erukkumcheḍi, Tam.). The stalks are soft and fibrous, and rubbing with them does not scratch the coin. The alkali which they contain, also, doubtless has its effect in removing the deposit from the lead.

As to the method by which the device was impressed on these leaden coins, Thomas states[1] that "the larger coins were obviously, in many cases, *cast*, but lead was alike so "soft in itself, and so readily made softer by heat, that we should be wrong to pronounce any "final opinion upon the actual methods of manipulation, which seem, however, to have "admitted of a superimposed, or otherwise, as it is *technically* termed, superstruck, secondary "impression. Whether this was effected by mere re-heating and the pressure of a hard clay "mould upon the surface of the original casting, it would be hard to say," . . . "That "mechanical *striking*, or the complete formation of a coin of two dies, was in vogue at this "coincident period, is proved by the smaller copper coins bearing the same legends and "devices as the leaden pieces, which, however, come out far more distinctly in their devices, "and sharper and more definite in their legends than the associate coins of the other metal. "The Śiṁha coins" . . . . . "furnish us with unusually definite examples of a practice "common in the early mintages of Southern India of designedly leaving the lower surface of "the piece *blank*. In these instances, the *lead* has seemingly been poured out, in a fluid "state, from a heated ladle, on to flat surfaces of stone or even wood, and then sealed with "the impress of the single authorized die." If moulds were used in casting these coins, they could not have been in the form usually understood by the term, that is, they could not have been sunk to a depth equal to the thickness of the coin, else we should invariably have found the device completely on and in the centre of the coin; but very seldom is it so. The outline

[1] *Ind. Antiq.*, vol. IX, p. 64.

of the coin also, would have taken a more regular form in the shape of the mould. In none of the coins obviously intended to be round, is a perfect circle seen. Some are of very irregular shape, while others have a protuberance on one side, as if the metal had been molten and oozed out on the one side on pressure being made by the upper die. The engraving, therefore, whether used as a mould, on to which the metal was poured and allowed to cool, or into whose shape it was forced, could only have had an impression of the device without an enclosing trough. The die used for the obverse, is usually of a size approaching to, though occasionally slightly larger than that of the coin. The case is different with the reverse, where large and small devices seem to have been used indiscriminately without reference to the size of the coin, or to the position the engraving on the reverse die occupies with the device on the obverse.

As to the question of the Śiṁha coins furnishing examples of the practice of leaving the reverse blank, the present specimens would seem to indicate that the absence of a device may in certain cases at least, be due to the coins being large and heavy, and that the device being raised in thin lines on a flat surface, had been worn off, while the coin was in use. Some of the larger horse coins have the reverse plain, apparently for the same reason. Three of the Śiṁha coins, for instance (Nos. 46, 47, and 50), yet retain traces of the Ujjain symbol. Another of these coins (No. 45) shows a *sunk* device, evidently *struck* with a punch.

The superstruck coins must go to prove that the dies were struck on cold metal; for, had the coins been heated, the original device would have been destroyed. Yet these coins retain both the original and secondary devices.

A consideration of what can be learned from an examination of this class of coin would seem to show that the process of minting, had followed one of two possible methods. It may have been to pour a given quantity of molten metal on to a plate engraved with an impression of the reverse and then press the metal into shape whith the obverse die, or, as seems more probable, to place a lump of cold metal of fixed weight and globular form, between a broad die plate containing an engraving of the reverse symbol, and a punch, of the intended diameter of the coin only, engraved with the obverse device, and strike on the latter till the approximate shape and thickness were attained. A few of the facts, which go to prove this, may be noted. When the obverse die has been struck to one side, a lumpy irregular rim caused by the bulging out of the metal over the edge of the die, appears on the other (see Nos. 40, 47, 57, &c.). On the reverse, no such rim ever appears, and however small the device may be with reference to the coin or, how much it may be placed to one side of it, the field around it is always flat. This shows that the reverse die had a considerable flat surface surrounding the engraving of the device, while the obverse die was only sufficiently broad to contain it. It seems more probable, therefore, that the metal may have been laid or poured on a somewhat *broad* surface, and struck or pressed with a *narrow* die than that the reverse process should have taken place. The Ujjain symbol, always in raised lines, is the device most commonly met with on the reverse sides of these coins. It is used in very diverse designs and sizes, as an inspection of those illustrated on plate XIII, will show. Some have a design which fits, or nearly fits the size of the coin, as on Nos. 1, 2, 5, 6, 35, 37, and 46, but in very few cases is the die in or near the centre of the coin; usually only a protion of the symbol appears. In others, the symbol is of a size slightly, or much larger than the coins on which it is used, as in Nos. 7, 13, 55 to 61, and 65 to 68. The obverse, on the other hand, is usually of a size to suit the coin, though it may not always appear in the centre of it. Sometimes again, a small symbol is struck on a large coin as in No. 52 or on a small coin as Nos. 8 and 17. As to the variations in the design of

ANDHRA COINS FROM GUḌIVÂḌA.

OBVERSE TYPES. PLATE XII.

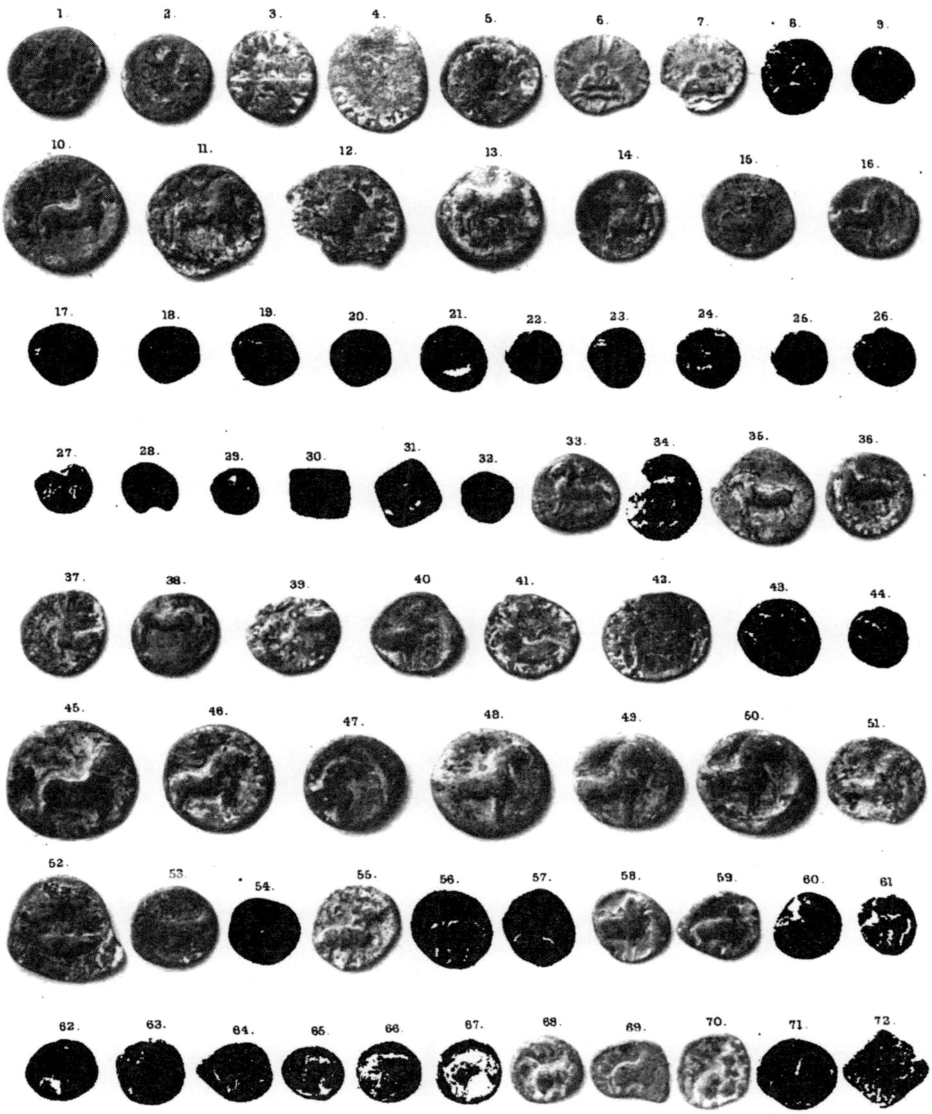

Photo-etching. Survey of India Offices. Calcutta. September 1893

FULL SCALE.

ANDHRA COINS FROM GUDIVÂḌA.

REVERSE TYPES.

PLATE XIII.

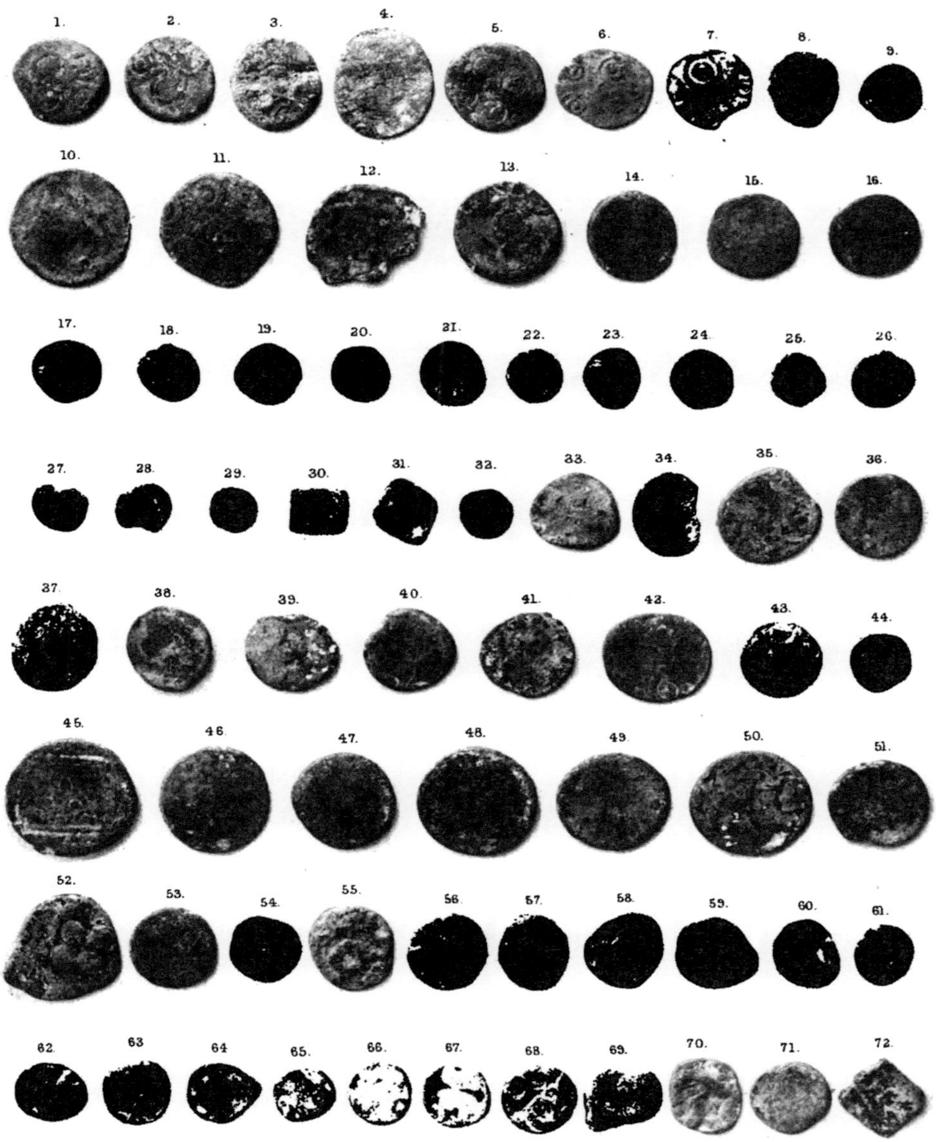

Photo-etching

Survey of India Offices, Calcutta, November 1893.

FULL SCALE.

the symbol, Nos. 1 to 5, 7, 13 and 37, though of different sizes, show one class with a dot in the centre, and two thin-lined circles surrounding it. No. 6 has the same figure, but the outer circle terminates in two prongs at the extremity of the arms. This, however, may perhaps be due to the coin having been bruised, or worn at that particular place. Other types are those in Nos. 8, 10, 11, 35, and 46, which have one broad lined circle around the dot. Solid circles appear on Nos. 52 and 53, but they may not originally have been so. Another class, as in Nos. 55, 56, 57, 60, 61, 65, 66, and 68, have no central dot, but only the central crossed lines prolonged into the centre of the circles. This feature is most distinct on No. 68. The broad lined symbols are of more archaic design than those of thin lines, and being found only on the more crudely stamped coins, would mark them of older date than the others. The coin last referred to (No. 68) also, has traces of other crossed lines, not at right angles, joining the outer segments of the circles, as if the die had been a large one with more than one series of four circles joined together by crossed lines, perhaps for impressing more than one coin at a time. On No. 55, for instance, there are traces of what appear six circles, and No. 63 has a lattice-work arrangement of lines with small circles at some of the intersections. No. 13 is a very distinct device, with a half moon fixed on the outer extremity of the one complete circle which shows on the coin. No. 17 also, has the half-moon, of the same radius as the circle to which it is attached. Some reverses, now apparently plain, or, nearly so, have before had devices stamped on them; thus on figures 10, 11, 12, 47, 50, &c., indistinct traces of the symbol appear. No. 45 has an unusual device, being a square of three sunk lines on each face, enclosing a number of dots and semi-circles. No. 70 has a curious device, the precise meaning of the design of which, it is difficult to discover. A number of the coins have inscriptions, but they are usually much worn and defaced, with only a few of the letters legible. Generally, only a part of the legend appears on one coin. The full inscription may sometimes be obtained by comparing several of the one kind.

In plates XII and XIII the coins have been arranged into a typical series according to the leading device they bear on the obverse. With only a comparatively small number of the coins inscribed; and even these, with only a few of the letters of the legend discernible, it would be unsatisfactory to attempt to arrange them otherwise. The former plate shows the obverse and the latter the reverse of the coins, in each case under the same number. Nos. 1 to 9 are chaitya coins, only one (No. 1) of which has the surmounting half-moon. Nos. 10 to 44 have the horse, either facing right or left. They are usually very sharply cut, especially some of the small coins, which have retained their clearness better than those of larger size. Nos. 45 to 51 are Śiṁha coins, all with the statant lion facing the right. Three varieties of the ship are shown on figures 52 to 54. The remainder are miscellaneous coins, generally of crude execution. It is sometimes difficult to discern exactly what animal some of these are intended to represent, but the principal device among them seems to be the elephant.

CHAITYA COINS.

No. 1. Lead. Round. Weight 74 grains.

Obverse.—Device slightly to left. Chaitya with three rows of inverted semi-circles surmounted by a half-moon. Below the pedestal a serpent in a wavy line.

Legend.—तमीपुतससरय.

tami-putasa saraya.

Reverse.—An Ujjain symbol of the same diameter as the coin. Design, dot enclosed in two circles.

No. 2. Lead. Round. Weight 68 grains.

Obverse.—Devico to right. Chaitya with two rows of semi-circles, and wavy serpent at foot.

Legend.—वस.

vasa.

Reverse.—Ujjain symbol. Same die as No. 1, but three-fourths only visible on top.

No. 3. Lead. Round. Weight 68 grains. Coin crushed by a line struck through middle of device.

Obverse.—A chaitya seemingly similar to No. 2.

Legend.—स . . . पुत.

sa . . . puta.

Reverse.—Ujjain symbol as in preceding; half of device on coin.

No. 4. Lead. Round. Weight 66 grains. Coin crushed thin to an oval shape.

Obverse.—Chaitya with two rows of semi-circles, and serpent at foot.

Legend.—पुतस—सिवा.

putasa—Śivâ.

Reverse.—Ujjain symbol as in preceding, half of device on left of coin.

No. 5. Lead. Round. Weight 78 grains.

Obverse.—Two-rowed chaitya, with serpent at foot.

Legend.—वासिटोपु.

vâ si tho-pu.

Reverse.—Ujjain symbol as in preceding; entirely on coin, but struck down towards lower edge.

No. 6. Lead. Round. Weight 32 grains. A thin coin.

Obverse.—Two-rowed chaitya, with serpent at foot.

Legend.—Illegible; traces of letters visible around.

Reverse.—Ujjain symbol slightly off left. Design three thin circles round dot. Outer circle terminates in prongs.

No. 7. Lead. Round. Weight 35 grains. Small piece broken off lower left side.

Obverse.—Two-rowed chaitya, with serpent at foot.

Legend.—Illegible; traces of letters around upper half.

Reverse.—Ujjain symbol as in No. 1, but with larger circles. Design larger than coin.

No. 8. Lead. Round. Weight 22 grains. A small coin.

Obverse.—A small two-rowed chaitya, with serpent at foot.

Legend.—Illegible.

Reverse.—Small Ujjain symbol to left. Design, dot and one circle.

No. 9. Lead. Round. Weight 17 grains.

Obverse.—A small two-rowed chaitya, with serpent at foot.

Legend.—Traces visible on top.

Reverse.—Device illegible.

The Horse facing right.

(Large Coins.)

No. 10. Lead. Round. Weight 120 grains. A large thick coin.

Obverse.—A boldly executed figure of a horse to the right, half-moon in the field. Rim raised, centre concave.

Legend.—सतकण.

satakana.

Reverse.—Ujjain symbol, with dot and one circle, much worn. Slightly less than coin, but struck towards right.

No. 11. Lead. Round. Weight 130 grains. A large thick coin.

Obverse.—Horse to the right, with half-moon in the field.

Legend.—सतकणस.

sataknasa.

Reverse.—Ujjain symbol as in No. 10, struck towards left.

No. 12. Lead. Round. Weight 115 grains. A fragment of a similar coin to No. 11.

Obverse.—Horse to the right, with half-moon in the field.

Legend.—गोतमिपुत.

Go tami-puta.

Reverse.—Device, the usual symbol, but nearly worn away.

No. 13. Lead. Round. Weight 122 grains. A thick coin of a slightly less diameter than those preceding.

Obverse.—A well raised horse to the right.

Reverse.—The half of an Ujjain symbol on the upper part of field. The figure, if complete, would slightly more than cover the coin. The one complete arm has two well raised circles around a central dot, with a half-moon on the outer extremity.

(Medium size Coins.)

No. 14. Lead. Round. Weight 55 grains.

Obverse.—Horse to the right. Field slightly concave.

Legend.—सिरि.

siri.

Reverse.—Faint traces of a large Ujjain symbol.

No. 15. Lead. Round. Weight 45 grains.

Obverse.—Horse to the right.

Legend.—सतस.

satasa.

Reverse.—Plain.

No. 16. Lead. Round. Weight 65 grains. A thick coin.

Obverse.—Horse to the right. Raised rim, and concave field.

Reverse.—Plain.

(*Small Coins.*)

Nos. 17, 18 and 19. Lead. Round. Weight 18, 11 and 14 grains. Three specimens of one class of coin. Thin.

Obverse.—A sharply cut figure of a horse to the right; an upright post with top and bottom cross-bars under the horse's head. A sun formed of a circle of dots surrounding a central dot, in the field.

Reverse.—Small Ujjain symbol on right, formed of a ball on the extremity of each of four crossed lines, and a semi-moon on the outer edge of the circle. Device shows clearly on No. 17, hardly visible on the others.

No. 20. Lead. Round. Weight 16 grains. A thicker coin than the three preceding.

Obverse.—Horse to the right. Portion of a rim underneath.
Reverse.—Two dots of a small Ujjain symbol visible on left.

No. 21. Lead. Round. Weight 28 grains. A similar coin to No. 20, but larger and thicker.

Nos. 22 and 23. Lead. Round. Weight of each, 11 grains.

Obverse.—Horse to the right.
Reverse.—Plain.

No. 24. Lead. Round. Weight 22 grains.

Obverse.—Horse to the right. Field slightly concave, with rim around.
Reverse.—Plain.

No. 25. Lead. Round. Weight 19 grains, similar to, but smaller than No. 24.

No. 26. Lead. Round. Weight 12 grains. Coin thin and bruised. Probably a specimen of Nos. 17, 18 and 19.

Obverse.—Horse to the right.
Reverse.—Plain.

No. 27. Lead. Round. Weight 6 grains. A fragment of a very thin coin.

Obverse and *Reverse.*—Same as the preceding.

No. 28. Lead. Round. Weight 8 grains. A very thin coin. Portion broken off lower side.

Obverse.—Horse to the right. A variant of No. 27. Difference visible in body and legs of the horse.
Reverse.—Bruised, and device indistinguishable.

No. 29. Lead. Round. Weight 4 grains. Very small and thin coin, variant of the preceding.

No. 30. Lead. Oblong. Weight 20 grains.

Obverse.—Horse to the right. Field circular concave.
Reverse.—Plain. Edges of coin slightly bevelled.

The Horse to the left.

(Small Coins.)

No. 31. Lead. Square with rounded corners. Weight 20 grains.

Obverse.—Horse to the left, with vertical post and cross-bars in front. Circular concave field. Device struck diagonally.

Reverse.—Bruised, with slight traces of Ujjain symbol.

No. 32. Lead. Round. Weight 9 grains. Small thin coin.

Obverse.—Clearly cut figure of horse to the left.

Reverse.—Plain.

(Medium size Coins.)

No. 33. Lead. Round. Weight 65 grains. Coin bruised out of shape.

Obverse.—Horse to the left. Dotted sun in the field.

Legend.—Illegible traces on right top.

Reverse.—Two dots of Ujjain symbol visible.

No. 34. Lead. Oval, with piece out of left side. Weight 49 grains.

Obverse.—Well raised horse to the left, with head broken away.

Legend.—Slight traces visible at bottom.

Reverse.—Portions of Ujjain symbol with dot and two circles; device, diameter of coin.

No. 35. Lead. Round with upper left edge flattened. Weight 71 grains.

Obverse.—Horse in high relief to the left.

Reverse.—Ujjain symbol slightly larger than coin, with dot and one circle.

No. 36. Lead. Round. Weight 63 grains.

Obverse.—Horse to the left.

Legend.—तस सि.

tasa si.

Reverse.—One circle of Ujjain symbol visible.

No. 37. Lead. Flattened round. Weight 48 grains.

Obverse.—Well raised horse to the left, with hind quarters off coin. Round object over back, probably a sun.

Legend.—कणस.

kaṇasa.

Reverse.—Ujjain symbol of size of coin. Two thin circles around dot.

No. 38. Lead. Round. Weight 65 grains.

Obverse.—Well raised horse to the left, with head off coin.

Legend.—तमिपु.

...tami-pu.

Reverse.—Traces of Ujjain symbol.

No. 39. Lead. Round. Weight 49 grains. Probably a specimen of No. 37.

Obverse.—Horse to the left with sun in the field. Field much indented.

Reverse.—Device illegible.

No. 40. Lead. Round. Weight 57 grains.

Obverse.—Horse to the left, with forepart off coin. Rim on the right. Seems the same die as No. 38.

Legend.—गोतमिपु.

Go tami-pu.

Reverse.—Traces of Ujjain symbol, much worn.

No. 41. Lead. Round. Weight 34 grains. A thin and bruised coin.

Obverse.—Horse to the left, with lower quarters off coin.

Legend.— . . . तमि . . . णस.

. . . tami . . . ṇasa.

Reverse.—Device illegible.

No. 42. Lead. Oval. Weight 45 grains. A "double-struck" coin.

Obverse.—Horse to the left. A circle over the horse's head is part of the super-struck Ujjain symbol. Surface flattened.

Legend.— . . . तकणस.

. . . takaṇasa.

Reverse.—Bruised, and device indistinguishable. A circle appears at the foot, and traces of what may be letters through centre of coin.

No. 43. Lead. Round. Weight 40 grains.

Obverse.—A horse seemingly, facing left. Device much worn.

Reverse.—Worn and indistinct.

No. 44. Lead. Round. Weight 18 grains. A small coin.

Obverse.—A horse (?) to the left.

Reverse.—Plain.

Śiṁha Coins.

No. 45. Lead. Round. Weight 218 grains.

Obverse.—A lion facing right.

Reverse.—A square, enclosed by three *sunk* lines on each of the sides. Inside the square, three tiers of sunk semi-circles with a dot inside each, are visible. The lowest tier has three, the second two, and the upper one. These may possibly represent a chaitya, but as the rest of the surface is worn, it is impossible to see whether the square may not have been completely filled in with these semi-circles.

No. 46. Lead. Round. Weight 132 grains.

Obverse.—Lion to the right, with tail curled over its back. Field concave.

Legend—समसे.

samase.

In some śiṁha coins from Amarâvati, described by Thomas[1] the legend is given as सकसकस *sakasakasa.* In the present specimen the second letter is clearly an म. The legend is close to the edge of the coin, and the vowel marks over the स, are uncertain. Two letters

[1] *Ind. Antiq.*, vol. IX, p. 46, 1880.

follow the second ब, but only the lower portion is visible. It is uncertain what they are, but they are not the terminal letters of the Amarâvati coins.

Reverse.—Ujjain symbol slightly less than coin, with dot and one circle, struck off top.

No. 47. Lead. Round. Weight 121 grains.

Obverse.—Forepart of lion to the right. Field sunk, with raised rim on right.

Legend.— Around right, illegible except letter स.

Reverse.—Faint traces of Ujjain symbol.

No. 48. Lead. Round. Weight 165 grains.

Obverse.—Lion to the right. Field slightly concave.

Reverse.—Plain.

No. 49. Lead. Round. Weight 150 grains.

Obverse.—Lion to the right, with hind quarters off coin. Field slightly concave.

Reverse.—Plain concave.

No. 50. Lead. Round. Weight 162 grains.

Obverse.—Lion to the right, with hind quarters off coin. Part of the tail appears over the back. In front is an upright line with a row of upward pointing branches on each side. A seemingly similar device has been described as consisting of triśulas,[1] but in the present case the figure more closely resembles a tree. The field is concave, and as the die has been struck to the left, a broad rim appears on the right.

Reverse.—Nearly plain, evidently been an Ujjain symbol.

No. 51. Lead. Round. Weight 81 grains.

Obverse.—A lion to the right, with tail over back. Field flat, without rim.

Reverse.—Plain.

SHIP COINS.

No. 52. Lead. Irregular round, with extension on the lower right. Weight 101 grains.

Obverse.—A ship resembling the Indian dhoni, with bow to the right. The vessel is pointed in vertical section at each end. On the point of the stem is a round ball. The rudder, in the shape of a post with spoon on end, projects below. The deck is straight, and on it are two round objects from which rise two masts, each with a cross tree at the top. Traces of rigging can be faintly seen.

Legend.— ण only legible.

Reverse.—A small Ujjain symbol on the right side, consisting of four central lines with four balls at the extremities.

No. 53. Lead. Round. Weight 65 grains.

Obverse.—A ship to the right. The device resembles that described under No. 52, but the features are not quite so distinct. The deck in this specimen is curved.

Reverse.—Traces of an Ujjain symbol, of the same size and form as in No. 52.

No. 54. Lead. Round. Weight 29 grains.

Obverse.—A device similar to the preceding, showing even more distinctly than No. 52. The rigging is crossed between the masts. On the right end of the vessel appear three balls, and under the side are two spoon-shaped oars.

Reverse.—Traces of an Ujjain symbol with dot and one circle.

---

[1] *Ibid.*, No. 18.

ELEPHANT AND OTHER COINS.

No. 55. Lead. Round. Weight 52 grains.

Obverse.—An animal facing the right, seemingly an elephant with trappings.

Legend.— . . . सरिवण.

. . . *sarivaṇa.*

Reverse.—Ujjain symbol, larger than coin; central cross lines prolonged into a broad lined circle. Traces of a succession of circles visible.

No. 56. Lead. Round. Weight 41 grains.

Obverse.—Device and legend similar to No. 55.

Reverse.—Device similar to No. 55, but with portions of four circles only on coin.

No. 57. Lead. Round and thick. Weight 41 grains.

Obverse.—Device low down on the coin showing rim on the top. Evidently the same animal as on the two preceding coins.

Legend.—Same as in No. 55, but differently placed with reference to the head of the elephant.

Reverse.—Similar to No. 56, but with less of the device struck on coin.

Nos. 58 and 59. Lead. Round. Irregular. Weight 41 and 57 grains. The former somewhat worn.

Obverse.—Elephant to the right.

Reverse.—One solid circle only of Ujjain symbol, in centre of coin No. 58, traces of four similar on No. 59.

No. 60. Lead. Round. Weight 22 grains. A small variety of No. 55. Symbol on reverse smaller than in No. 55, &c.

Nos. 61 and 62. Lead. Round. Weight, each 22 grains.

Obverse.—A crude figure of an elephant to the right.

Reverse.—Device similar to preceding.

No. 63. Lead. Round. Weight 32 grains.

Obverse.—Animal, probably an elephant facing the right.

Reverse.—Four lines crossed diagonally with an almost solid circle at two of the intersections.

No. 64. Lead. Round with projection on left. Weight 18 grains. Thin.

Obverse.—Elephant to the right.

Reverse.—Device illegible.

No. 65. Lead. Round. Weight 14 grains.

Device on obverse similar to preceding. The reverse is similar to No. 56, but smaller.

No. 66. Lead. Round. Weight 26 grains.

Obverse.—Elephant to the left.

Reverse.—Ujjain symbol larger than coin; same design but smaller than No. 56, &c.

No. 67. Lead. Round. Weight 34 grains.

Obverse.—Device uncertain, probably an elephant to the right.

Reverse.—Traces of a device similar to No. 66.

No. 68. Lead. Round. Weight 45 grains.

***Obverse.*—Elephant to the right.**
***Legend.*—Illegible.**
***Reverse.*—Similar to No. 66, but larger.**

No. 69. Lead. Irregular shape. Weight 51 grains.

***Obverse.*—Animal to the right, probably an elephant.**
***Legend.*—Illegible.**
***Reverse.*—Traces of a small Ujjain symbol.**

No. 70. Lead. Round. Weight 41 grains.

***Obverse.*—Device indistinguishable, bears a slight resemblance to No. 57.**
***Legend.*—सिरिरु (द).**
Siri Ru (da).
***Reverse.*—Device indistinguishable.**

No. 71. Lead. Round. Weight 35 grains.

***Obverse.*—An animal to the right, perhaps a horse.**
***Legend.*—Illegible.**
***Reverse.*—Plain.**

No. 72. Lead. Square. Weight 30 grains.

***Obverse.*—A crude representation of an animal, probably a horse, facing left. Device struck diagonally.**

***Reverse.*—Two lines at right angles, with curved lines at the extremities.**

CHAPTER XIII.

GHAṆṬAŚÂLÂ.

EXCAVATION AT THE STÛPA.

A village in the Tsallâpalli Zamindâri, thirteen miles west of Masulipatam.

The Buddhist mound at this place was one of those noted by Mr. Boswell in his reports to Government in 1870–71.

The mound is known as Lañja dibba; and stands in the fields on the north-east of the village. It is circular in shape, and measures about 112 feet in diameter and 23 feet in height. Brick walls and black mud appear on the surface.

The cultivated fields extend close up to, and in parts encroach on the slope of the mound. On one side, part of a palmyra palm tope grows on the lower part of it.

The excavations, recently conducted in the mound, show the remains to be those of a Buddhist stûpa, of a date probably a few years subsequent to the later works at Amarâvati. The upper part of the building is away; but the foundations, with such portions of the upper walls as extend up to the surface of the mound, remain intact. These show an arrangement of plan not hitherto met with in any of those examined in South India. (Pl. XIV, fig. 2.)[1]

The Ghaṇṭaśâlâ stûpa has a cube of solid brickwork in the centre, measuring 10 feet square. Enclosing it is a hollow chamber, measuring 19 feet square, with walls 3 feet 4 inches thick. It is connected with the central cube by a cross wall, 2 feet 4 inches thick, which runs out at right angles from each face of the latter. Outside it, is a circular wall 3 feet 6 inches thick and 55 feet 10 inches in exterior diameter. The four cross walls above referred to, are continued out to join this circle; the four walls also, of the hollow square are produced out—two from each corner—but with a thickness of 2 feet 4 inches, till they touch the circle. Beyond, and concentric with this inner circle, at a distance from it, of 11 feet 7 inches, is a massive circular wall measuring 18 feet 3 inches thick. Its outer surface is shown, by a chunam facing which still remains on a few of the lower courses. On the south, 2 feet in height is left; it is perfectly vertical. The space between it, and the inner circle is divided into sixteen cells by a like number of walls which radiate from the centre, and connect the two circles. These walls are 2 feet 4 inches thick, and twelve of them branch out from the inner circle from the points where it is intersected by the before-noted inner cross walls. The thirty-two hollow chambers thus formed in the interior of the stûpa are filled with firmly-packed black mud. The additional four walls are placed opposite the four corners. Around the outer circular wall, is a stylobate 5 feet 7 inches broad and 4 feet 6 inches high. It is broad enough for a procession-path; and has doubtless formed the lower one of a series of such. Its wall leans forward at a considerable angle, and the offset on the top slopes out and downwards. It is unbroken on all sides except the east. It was excavated all around, except where the palm tope prevented it; and no marbles were found standing in position against any portion of it. The quarters of this base, which face the four cardinal points, have each projected 5 feet, for a length of 17 feet 6 inches. The projection on the north side is nearly complete; on the south, a few of the lower courses remain; on the east it is entirely away; and of that on the west, a few traces remain. On the face of the wall,

---

[1] The shading indicates the walls laid bare by excavation. The remaining walls can be traced on the surface of the mound.

PLATE XIV

GHAṆṬAŚÂLÂ.

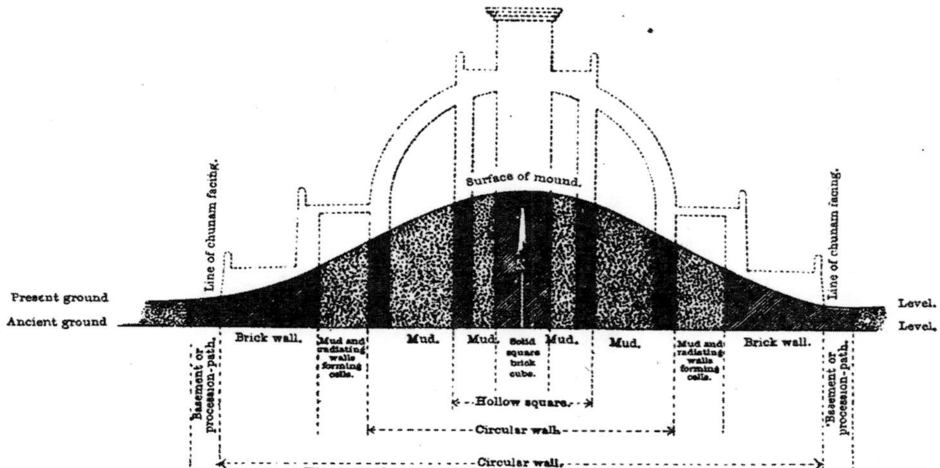

Fig. 1. Section. Dotted lines indicate assumed outline of building.

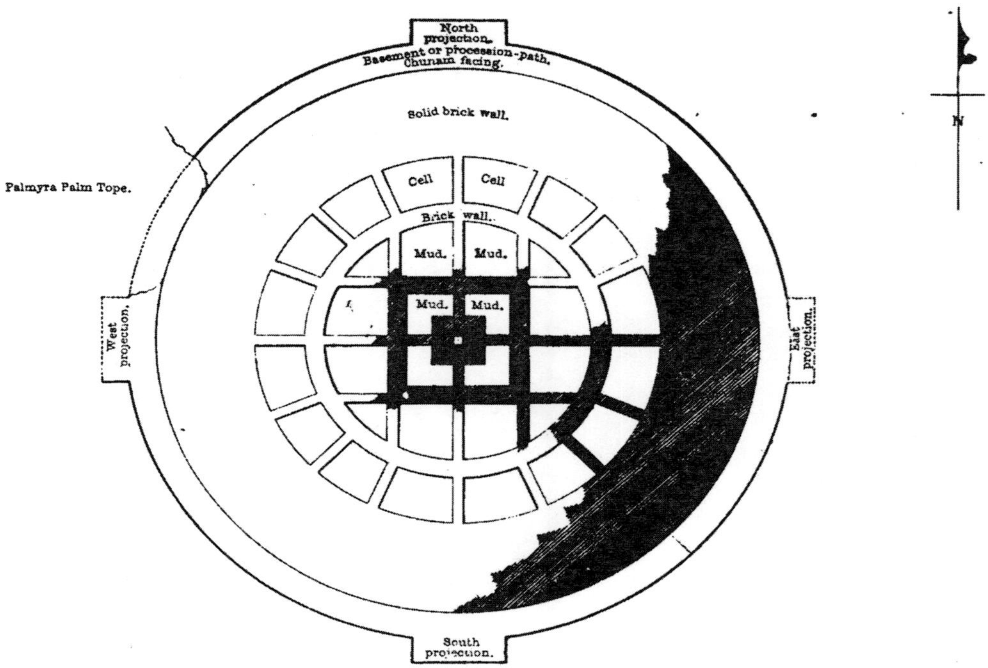

Scale of 5 10 20 30 40 50 100 130 Feet

Photo., S. I. O., Calcutta.

GHAṆṬAŚÂLÂ.

A MARBLE ŚRÎPÂDA.

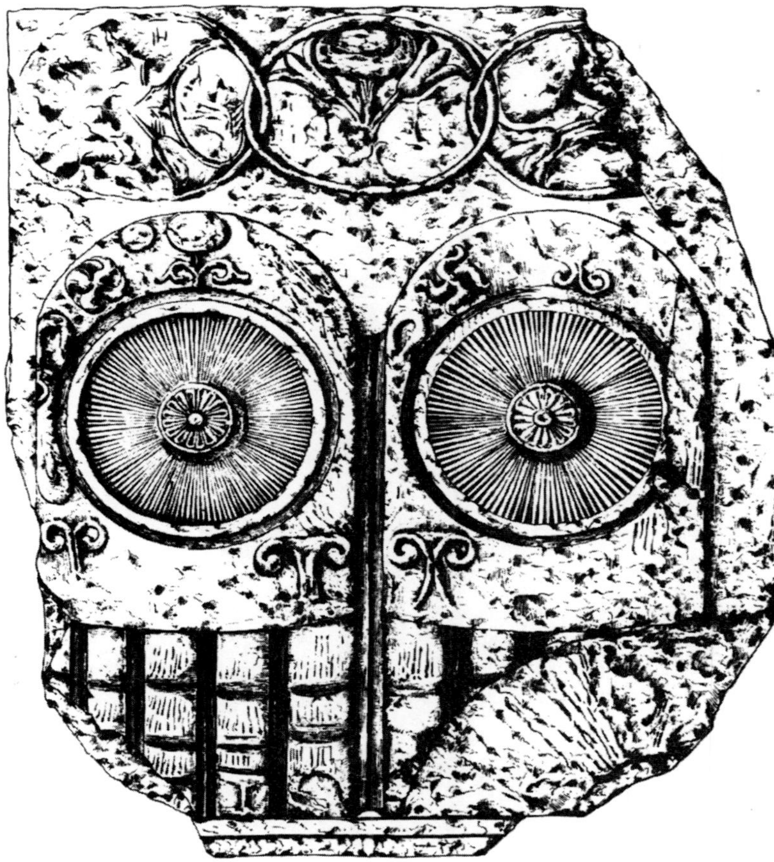

Scale of 12" 9" 6" 3" 1 Foot.

GHAṆṬAŚÂLÂ.

FRAGMENT OF THE OUTER FACE OF A RAIL PANEL.

Scale of 0 6 12 Inches.

Photo., S. I. O., Calcutta.

GHAṆṬAŚÂLÂ

Relic Casket.

Fig. 1. Outer Casket.

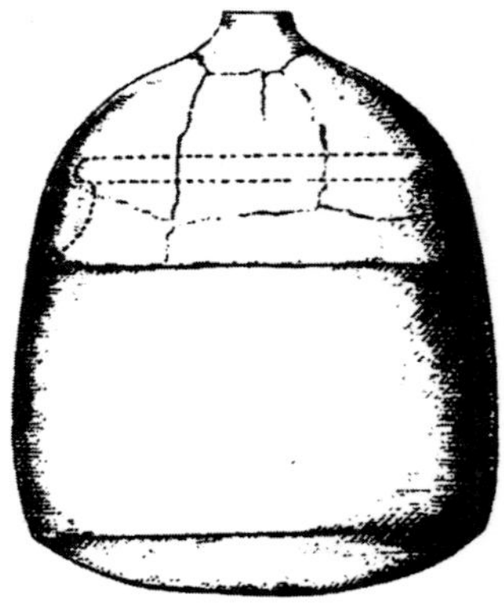

Fig. 2. Section.

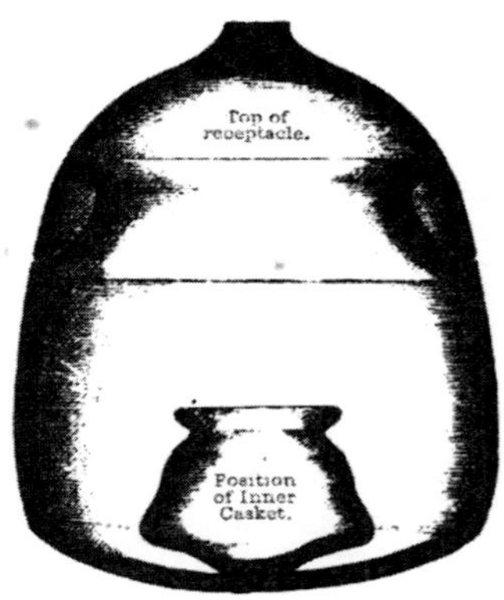

Fig. 3. Inner Casket.

Scale of 1 2 3 4 5 6 Inches.

Photo., S. I. O. Calcutta.

over and opposite the south projection, a mass of chunam was observed. This seems to have been an ascending stair, or other feature: it may also have existed at the other three projections. Around the basement, and now from 4 to 6 feet underground, is a brick floor. It is much broken up, and it is now impossible to tell what its breadth may have been, or whether a marble rail stood on the outer edge of it. Some marbles were found lying in the earth outside the south projection: only two are carved. A number of these were small plain slabs, some with a splay on one edge.

One panel is carved with the Śrîpâḍa or Buddha's footprint. (Pl. XV.) Three corners of the slab are broken off. It is similar to some which were found at Amarâvati. The carving is much weather-worn. Behind the heels is a lotus flower scroll. On the soles of the feet are two chakras, "the two beautiful brilliant white wheels with a thousand rays" described by the legends which enumerate the thirty-two personal marks of Buddha.[1] Around the chakras is a variety of emblems. They are much worn; the svastika with bent arms, and the triśula, can be clearly distinguished; only traces of others appear. The other carved stone is a fragment of a top rail panel (pl. XVI). It is plain on the back. It has the half of a chakra mounted on a pedestal, with a portion of a flowing scroll on the one side of it. In the top panel of a detached rail, with carving on both sides, the scroll is placed on the outer face. The height of this stone is insufficient for such a rail as would have been placed around this building. It is more suited to such as would be found on the edge of a raised procession-path around the dome; and as such it may have been used.

The brickwork on the surface of the square in the centre of the stûpa appeared quite solid, and was laid in parallel courses. It extended thus for a depth of 3 feet. At that point, in the centre, was the top of a well, 9 inches square, filled with earth. Among the first earth removed, were pieces of a broken chatti, and the following articles which, apparently, it had at one time contained,—a small lead coin $\frac{3}{8}$th inch square, with an illegible symbol on one side; a pentagonal blue and white crystal bead $\frac{9}{16}$th inch long; and three small beads. Scattered around among the earth—and which had evidently been placed with the same purpose as were the gold flowers around the small caskets at Bhaṭṭiprôḷu—was a quantity of red, white and blue pieces of crystal quartz. Just below these, was a small red earthenware chatti, 4½ inches in diameter and height. It has a semi-circular lid with a small knob on the top. (Pl. XVII, figs. 1 and 2.) It was filled with fine black earth. In the bottom stood a small glazed chatti, made of a material resembling stoneware. It is 1¾ inches in height, with a diameter of 2¼ inches. (fig. 3.) In it were—two small pieces of bone or coral (?); a white hexagonal crystal bead, $\frac{5}{8}$th inch long; five small round beads; a flat mother-of-pearl bead; six small pearls; two pieces of yellow crystal (quartz?); two bits of gold leaf, one of them cut as a flower with eight petals; and some bits of a mineral like that found in the third casket at Bhaṭṭiprôḷu (silicate?).

The small well in the centre of the stûpa gradually increased in size, till, at 13 feet from the surface, it was 2 feet 6 inches square. For the lower half of that depth it was filled with clay. The well there, was closed with a brick. Below that, the well was 9 inches and 12 inches square, each alternate course, down to the foundations, 26 feet from the summit of the mound. This portion also was packed with clay. There were no other relics. The foundations rest on sand. The various sizes of the openings of each course, in a portion of the well, is a feature also observed at Bhaṭṭiprôḷu. The bricks used in the central walls at Ghaṇṭaśâlâ are of very inferior material. It is difficult to find a perfect brick among

[1] Burgess: *Amar. and Jagg. Stûpas*, p. 97.

them; the majority are fractured, evidently by pressure of the mass of masonry which stood above them.

A few of the large numbers of marbles, which must have adorned the building, have been preserved in this and adjoining villages. These include piers; bases or capitals; an umbrella; carved rail; stûpa slabs; and some other slabs now cut with modern sculptures. The remainder have probably been gradually removed by the villagers when lime was required for building. The chief reason for the preservation of these others seems to have been their adaptibility to some useful purpose. Thus some of the piers are set up as boundary posts, an inscribed one stands in the temple, and the priests try to assert that it was found on the spot. The chief reason of its retention there, seems to be that, through the ancient inscription, a claim of antiquity can be made for the temple, itself a modern building. The moulded bases are utilized as grain mortars; while one of the stûpa slabs, and those with modern carved deities are worshipped.

GHAṆṬAŚÂLÂ.

MARBLE PANEL AT BAUDDHA VANAM.

Scale of 12" 9" 6" 3" 1 2 3 4 5 Feet.

Photo., S. I. O., Calcutta.

GHAṆṬAŚÂLÂ.

MARBLE PIER.

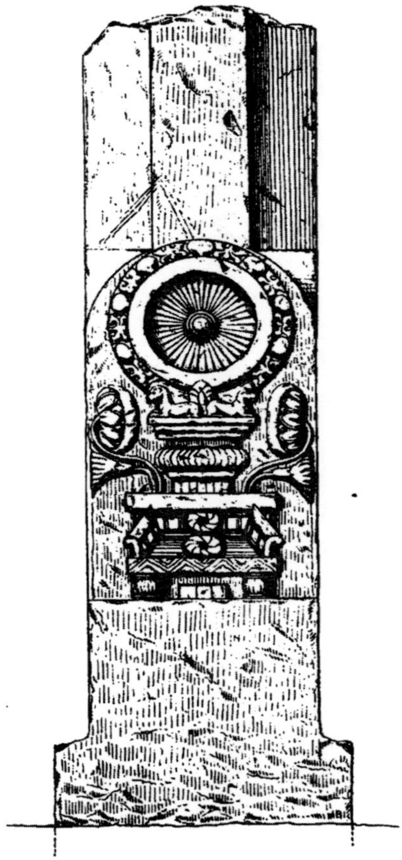

Plan.

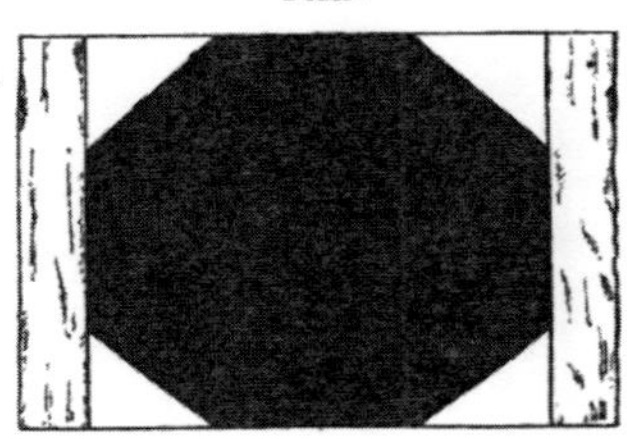

Scale of 12 9 6 3 . 1 2 3 4 5 Feet.

Photo., S. I. O., Calcutta.

GHAṆṬAŚÂLÂ.

Inscribed Marble Pier.

(Inscriptions not shewn on drawing.)

Plan.

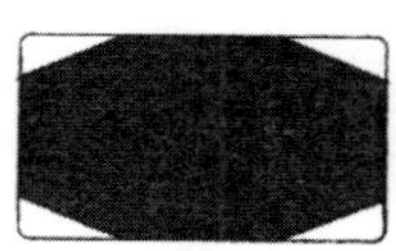

Scale of 12" 9" 6" 3" 0 1' 2' 3' 4' 5 Feet.

Photo., S. I. O., Calcutta.

CHAPTER XIV

PIERS.

Plate XVIII.

The carved stone represented, stands fixed in the ground under a tree in the parchari near Bauddha-vanam, on the west of Ghaṇṭaśâlâ. It is carved on the front and the right side; the other side and back are plain. A portion of the top has been broken off. The carving is in bas-relief, with the background but slightly sunk. The front panel has a vase at the foot from which spring varied grouped clusters of lotus and other flowers, and leaves in tiers above each other. The narrow panel on the side has an arrangement of the same ornament. The design is somewhat similar in general effect to one on the post of the northern gate at Sâñchi.[1]

Plate XIX.

This pier stands fixed in the ground at the Polimêradibba, or boundary mound. The top of the shaft is broken away: the portion that remains is octagonal. The base is square, with carvings on two opposite sides. The side represented has a throne, on which lie two lotus flowers. Behind it, two lotus flowers branch out on each side; while above it, rises a pedestal, which supports a chakra. A triśula ornament surrounds the wheel. The carving on the other side has been of similar design; but it has been nearly destroyed. The shaft over is octagonal. Four other fragments of piers stand beside this one. A few yards to the north of these, and close to the adjoining parchari, a small square uncarved pier is set up under a tree.

Plate XX.

This pier has been erected in the Jalatêśvara temple. The top and bottom are oblong; and the centre of the shaft a flat octagon. Curved stop-chamfers join the angle splays with the corners of the upper and lower rectangular portions of the pier. On the two broad faces, above and under the octagon, are semi-circular lotus-carved discs; each has traces of a carved horizontal band across its diameter: these discs do not appear on the two narrow sides. On the lower portion of the side of the pier opposite to that represented on the plate,—or facing the west, as it at present stands in the temple—is a long inscription in old Telugu characters. On the north side is another similar. On the south side are two inscriptions, the upper in Pali, and the lower in old Telugu.

[1] *Ind. and East. Arch.*, pl. 35.

CHAPTER XV.

BASES AND CAPITALS.

Plates XXI to XXV.

The square moulded stone shown in plate XXI is kept in a Brahman pûjâri's house near the Śiva temple; it is used as a grain mortar. The mouldings are devoid of ornament.

A finely carved circular band lies at a well near the stûpa. (Pl. XXII.) It is pierced with a cylindrical hole through the centre. In section it is a torus, with three bands of ornament around it. The lowest has a row of lotus leaves; the top has a series of drooping wreaths fixed with rosettes: while the central band has a procession of groups of domestic and wild animals. Each group is headed by the elephant, behind it follow the goat and tiger; cow and deer; horse and lion; the buffalo and the boar.

Plate XXIII shows a circular moulded stone with a rectangular hole cut through the centre. It lies near a well in the Śiva temple, and is used for beating clothes while they are being washed.

Another similar stone is square, with two steps moulded along the edges, and a circular fillet on the top. It is pierced with a cylindrical hole. It is used as a base to the dvajastambha in front of the Gramadêva temple. (Pl. XXIV.)

Plate XXV.

The plate represents a chhatra or umbrella, which is now kept in a Brahman pûjâri's house near the Śiva temple. The top is flat, and rounded around the edge. On the under side of the rim, is a plain fillet, pierced with eight small holes at equal spaces through its inner edge. These holes have probably been for suspending chains or bells. In the centre is a square socket-hole with a raised circular ledge around it. From this point, beaded rays radiate outwards to the rim. The umbrella is similar in size to one found at Amarâvati. It is too small to have been placed on the centre of the summit of the dome. Some of the Amarâvati stûpa slabs represent smaller umbrellas grouped around the great surmounting one; and also another over the central of the five columns placed against each of the four cardinal faces of the base of the dome. This stone may have been placed in either of these subordinate positions.

A similar stone has been removed to, and fixed as a seat in the floor of a house in Dêvarkôṭa. It is 3 feet 8 inches in diameter, and 6 inches thick above the floor. A square socket-hole is cut in the centre. The people objected to its being moved; so it could not be ascertained whether there were carvings on the under side.

PLATE XXI.

GHAṆṬAŚÂLÂ.

A MOULDED MARBLE.

Top

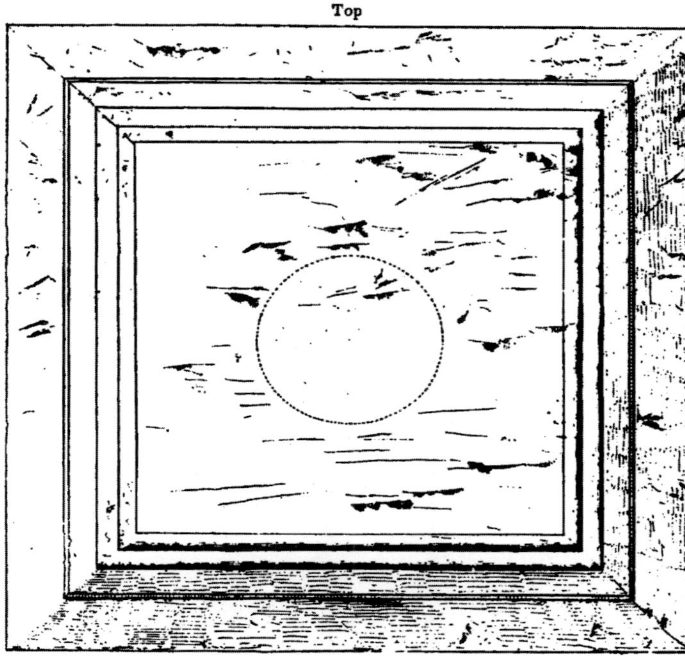

Side

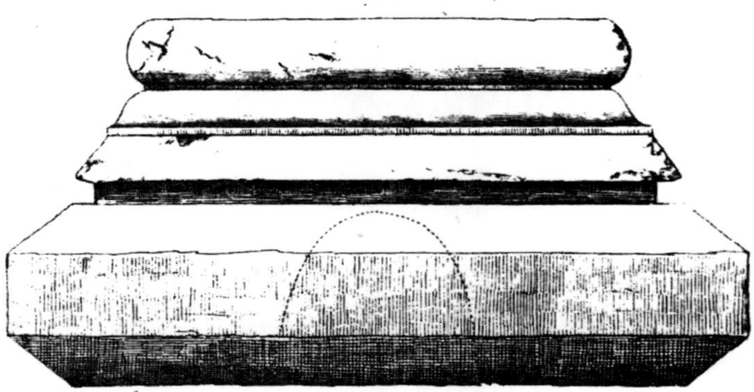

Scale of 12" 9" 6" 3" 1 Foot.

A CIRCULAR CARVED MARBLE.

Side.

Top.

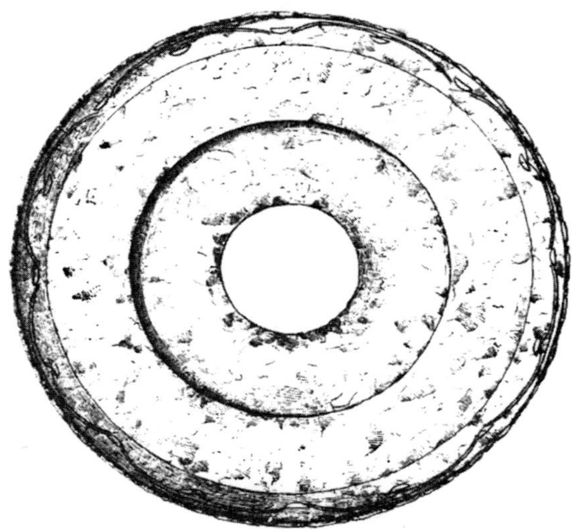

Scale of 12 9 6 3 1 2 Feet.

Litho., S. I. O. Calcutta

GHAṆṬAŚÂLÂ.

A Circular Moulded Marble.

Top

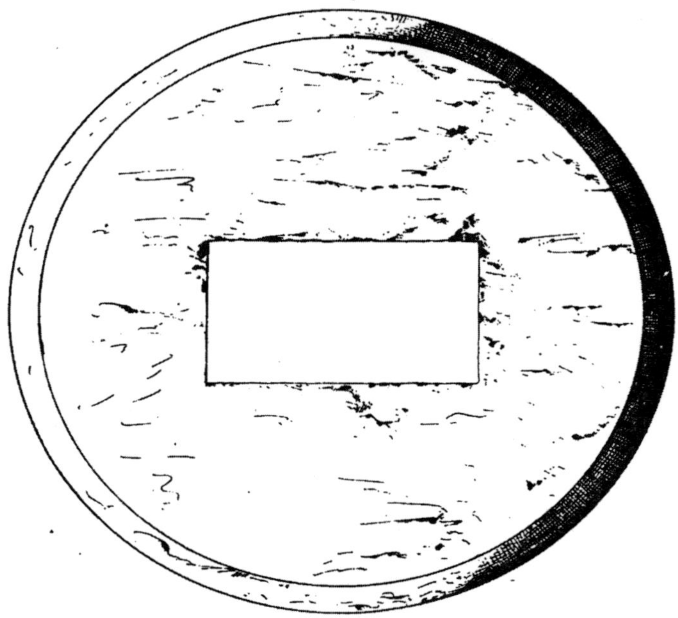

Side

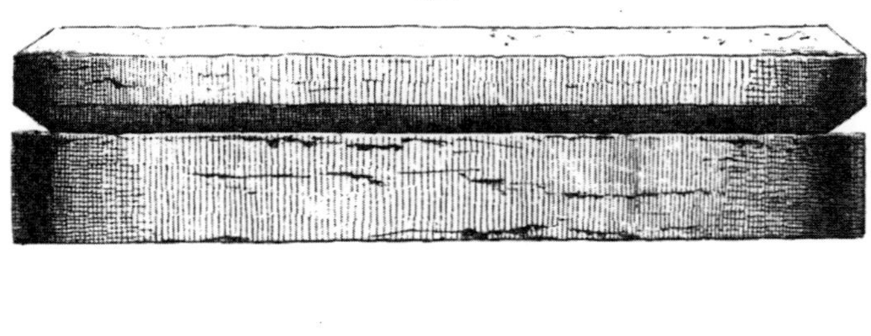

Scale of 12 9 6 3 0 1 2 Feet.

Photo.-S. I. O., Calcutta.

GHAṆṬAŚÂLÂ.

A. Square and Circular Marble.

Side

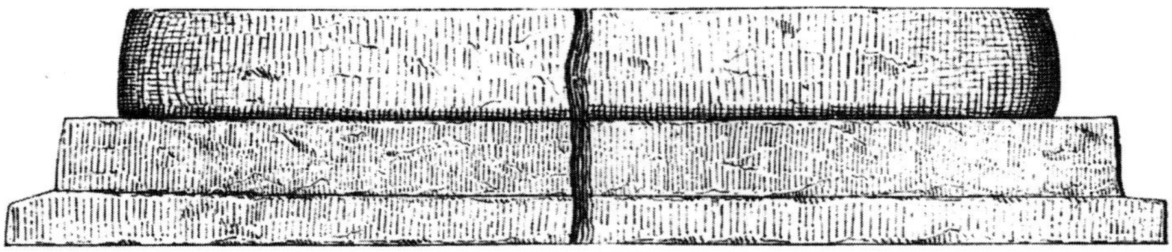

Top

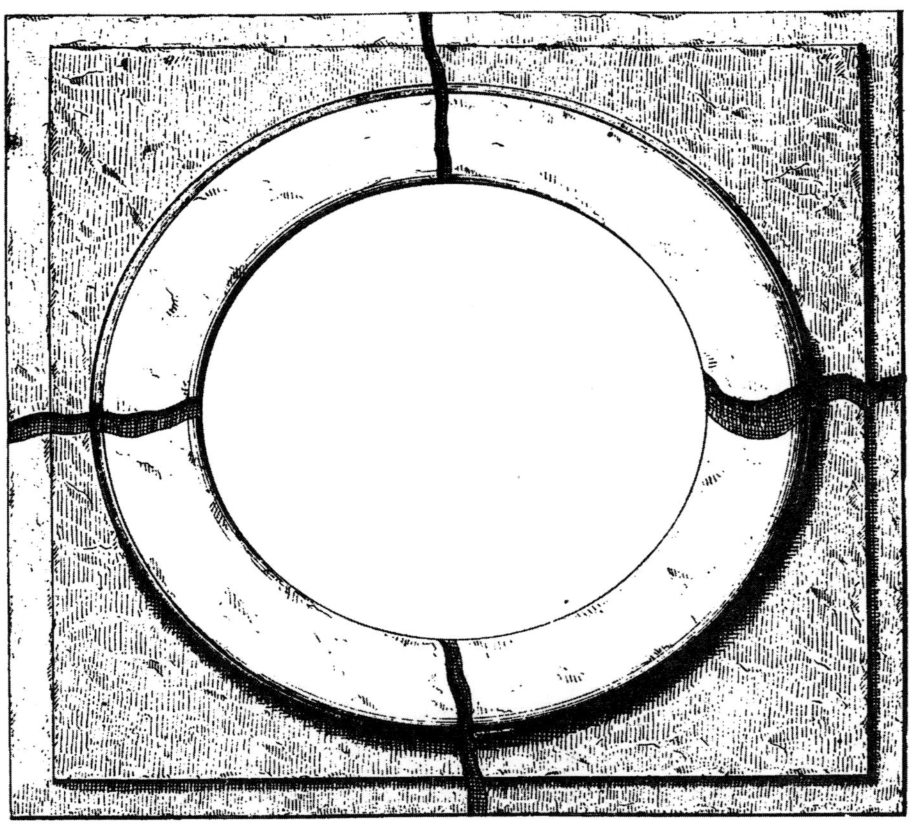

Scale of 0 3 6 9 12 Inches.

Photo. S. I. O., Calcutta.

GHAṆṬAŚÂLÂ.

Marble Umbrella.

Section.

Plan of under surface.

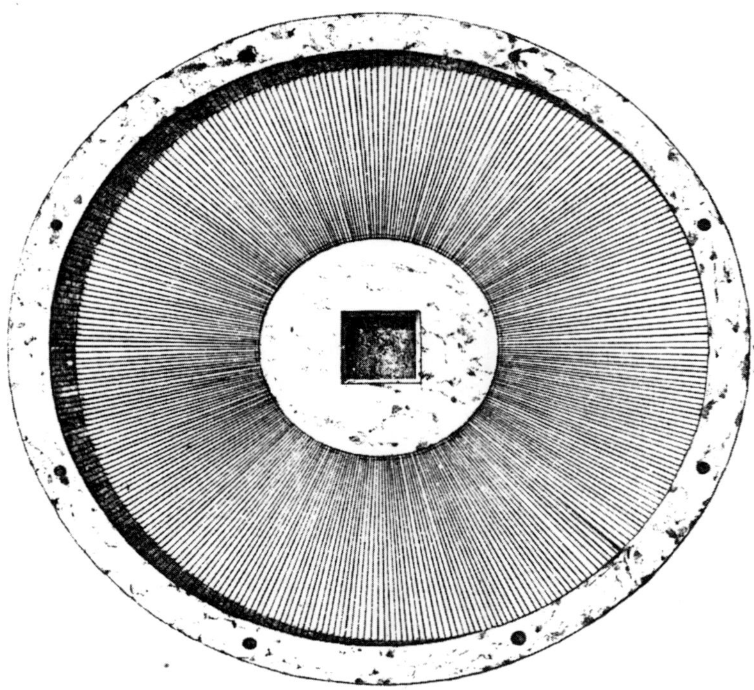

Scale of 12" 9" 6" 3" 0 1 Foot.

Photo., S. I. O., Calcutta.

GHAṆṬAŚÂLÂ.

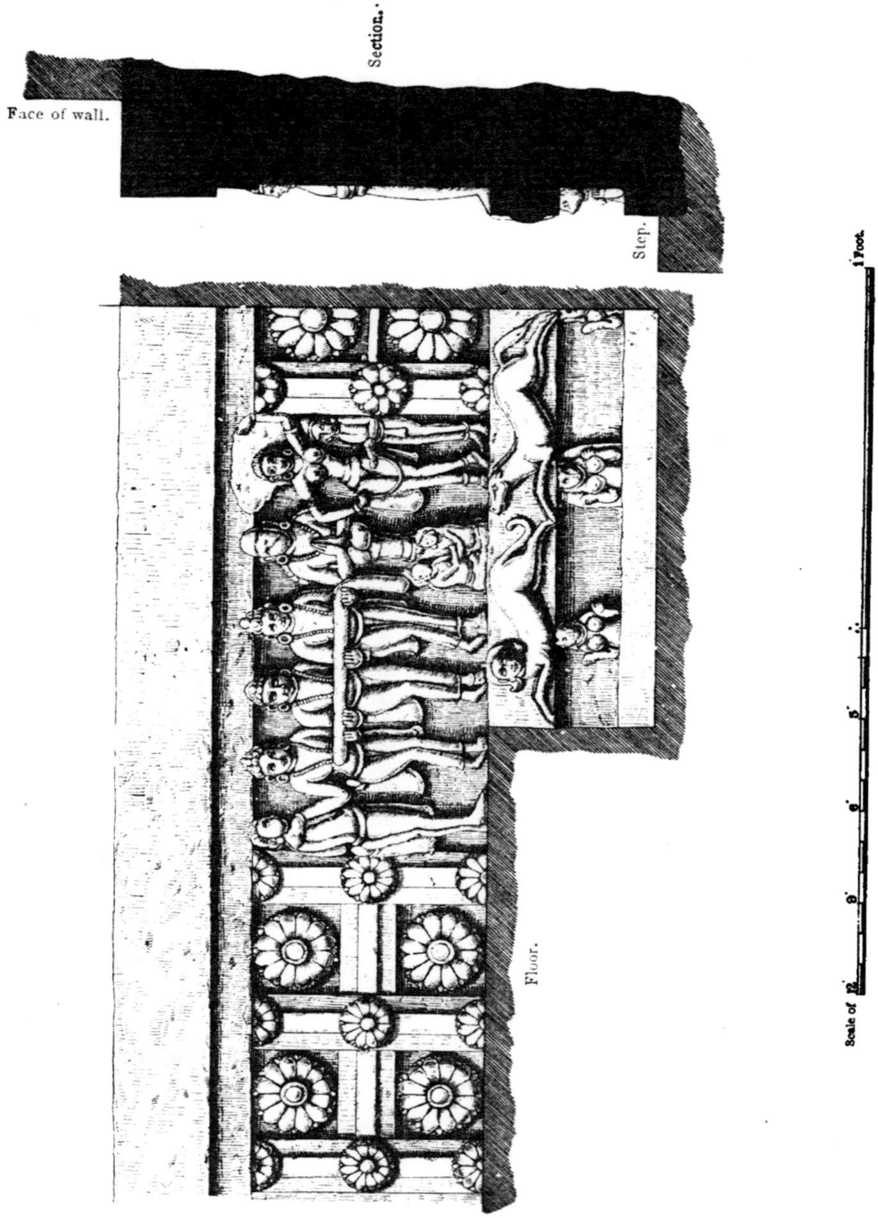

A Marble Rail Panel.

Photo., S. I. O., Calcutta.

GHAṆṬAŚÂLÂ.

PLATE XXVII.

A MARBLE STÛPA SLAB.

Scale of 12 9 6 3 1 2 3 Feet.

Litho., S. I. O., Calcutta.

Marble Slab, now at Râmanagaram.

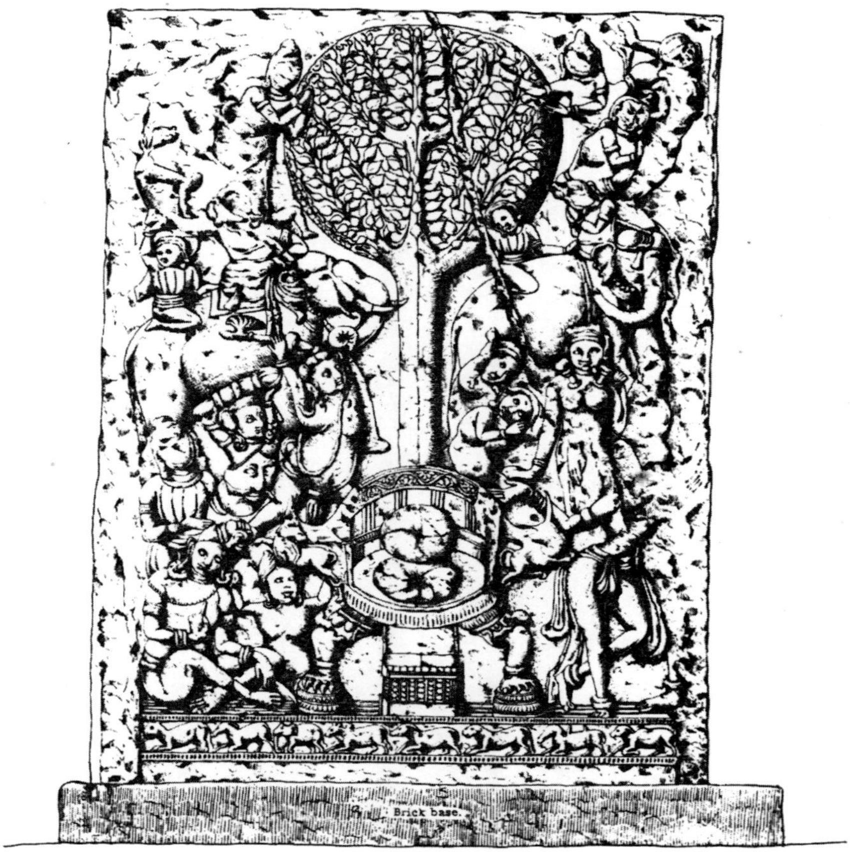

Scale of 12 9 6 3 0 1 2 3 Feet.

Litho., S. I. O., Calcutta.

CHAPTER XVI.

SLABS FROM THE STÛPA.

Plate XXVI represents a panel now fixed against a wall behind some images in the Jalatêśvara temple. It shows the posts, lotus discs and cross-bars of a rail. An open space, seems to be the gate in which a number of offering-bearing worshippers are entering. Below is a frieze with a horse, and an animal with a human head. This band evidently goes right along under the panel, but is sunk into the ground. Underneath, are a number of figure brackets. The slab seems to have been one of those which formed the parapet around one of the upper procession-paths.

Plate XXVII is a fine slab with the representation of a stûpa. It now stands in the road against the court wall of the Śiva temple. It presents no material difference from others found at Amarâvati and Pedda Gañjâm. Those from the latter place were found standing in position against the face of the basement. It is likely that this would be similarly placed. A statue of Buddha with worshippers around, occupies the principal panel inside the represented gateway. Over is the usual group of five pillars. On the top of the central of these piers, will be observed the remains of the umbrella, before alluded to. The projecting side gates are shown on each wing. Outside the front gateway are worshippers, with attendant dwarfs bearing offerings. The building is ornamented with sculptured panels from base to summit. The two upper corners of the slab are broken.

A finely sculptured slab (pl. XXVIII) now stands in the road in the village of Râmanagaram (Râmagrâma). It is worshipped by some of the villagers at certain seasons. It represents the worship of the sacred bodhî tree. At the trunk of the tree is a throne, bearing two lotus blossoms. The seat is supported on two legs with lion claws, raised on two carved cushioned bases. The whole space on both sides is filled with worshippers. On each side is an elephant, one facing to, and the other facing from the tree. The drivers and riders on their backs, turn to and worship the tree. Some bear offerings, and others sit in adoration around the foot. A figure on the left has a curious mask on the breast, precisely similar to some on the slabs from Peḍḍa Gañjâm. The heavy bracelets and anklets on the women is a noteworthy feature, and the great ornaments through the ear lobes of one, standing by the side of the tree, specially so. Under the slab, is a band with eight animals, showing the lion, deer, elephant, bullock, goat, tiger, horse and buffalo.

A fragment of a slab from the base of the stûpa is in a field near the brick mound subsequently described as on the boundaries of Dêvarakôṭa. It is plain, with a carved pilaster on one edge.

CHAPTER XVII.

MARBLE SLABS WITH MODERN SCULPTURES.

Plates XXIX to XXXII.

These plates show marble slabs that have been defaced and resculptured with Hindu deities. The first represents a fairly cut figure of Narasiṁha; the others are very coarsely carved; they are Bhairava, Sarasvati, and Rati. They stand in the Śiva temple.

The crude carving displayed on these slabs is in marked contrast to the style of the sculpture which was most probably hewn off to make way for them, if we may judge from such examples of the latter as have survived. They are examples of one of the three methods employed in the disposal of the matchless works of art which these buildings so abundantly produced.

If a slab was required for an image, the mound was dug into. Any found bearing sculptures with some remote resemblance to a Hindu deity were retained and set up for worship. Other sculptures were ruthlessly hewn off. Slabs, piers, or other details—it was immaterial whether they were moulded, carved, sculptured or plain—not so required or convertible, were hacked to pieces and made into mortar. These methods mark the popular appreciation of the finest works of art the country has produced. They have ever been open to the disposal of any one so inclined; and it should not be forgotten that many, probably the majority of them, continue so to be at the present time. Where the mounds are preserved for scientific investigation, this barbaric vandalism is effectually stopped; where they are not so, it is liable at any time to proceed unchecked.

GHAṆṬAŚÂLÂ.

IMAGE OF NARASIṀHA ON A MARBLE SLAB.

Scale of [illegible] 1 2 Feet.

Photo., S. I. O. Calcutta.

GHAṆṬAŚÂLÂ.

IMAGE OF BHAIRAVA ON A MARBLE SLAB.

Scale of 12" 9" 6" 3" 1 Foot.

Photo, S. I. O., Calcutta.

GHAṆṬAŚÂLÂ.

IMAGE OF SARASVATI ON A MARBLE SLAB.

Scale of 12 9' 6' 3' 1 Foot.

Photo., S. I. O., Calcutta.

PLATE XXXII

GHAṆṬAŚÂLÂ

IMAGE OF RATI ON A MARBLE SLAB.

Scale of 0" 6" 12" Inches.

Photo, S. I. O., Calcutta.

CHAPTER XVIII.

THE DESIGN OF THE STŪPA.

The design of the building may, according to the plan (pl. XIV, fig. 2) have been either of three forms. The first probable plan is that of an ancient small stûpa, represented by the inner circular wall, which had been encased in a larger and more modern dome. Some of the stûpas in Ceylon are admittedly in this form. Secondly, the building may have originally been a great dome springing from the line of the chunam facing on the top of the basement. The interior walls would, with it, have been placed to strengthen the dome. The third is, that the inner circle represents the original dome, while the walls outside it are the foundations of procession paths around it.

Against the first, is the fact that the wall of the inner circle is perfectly vertical for its present height, and in parts leans outwards. Had it been as assumed, the dome would not have been stilted in this way; some trace of the inward curve of the roof would, certainly at this height, have shown itself. The curve would have been started from a point at or about the level of a low surrounding basement, some few feet above the level of the ground. The builders also, of the encasing dome, would not, except at the cardinal points, have known to space the radiating walls so as to have them exactly opposite the cross walls in the interior of the inner circle. Moreover, the junctions of the inner circle, with the radiating walls outside it show no vertical open joint.

Against the second supposition of a large outer dome, is the great and unnecessary thickness of the outer ring, 18 feet 3 inches exclusive of the outside basement. This breadth is entirely out of proportion to any other of the stûpas in the district. The inner walls also show a distinct design, which would be unnecessary, and unlikely, if they were simply placed as interior supporting walls.

The third design which the plan suggests, seems the most probable of the three. It is that of some other stûpas which will now be alluded to. With no adjacent examples of its class with which to compare it, some difficulty might arise in realizing what its design may have been. There are, however, some similar buildings still existing in Ceylon and further India, which supply the necessary information. Their analogous plan would strongly suggest that this building had been designed on lines similar to them. Their chief peculiarity is a succession of circular terraces, concentric with, and rising in flights up to a dome in the centre. A second feature, is the presence in these circular galleries, of small chambers used either as cells for monks or niches for statues. It will conduce to clearness of comparison, if a brief reference to those others is made. The dâgoba at Ruanwelli in Ceylon (cir. B.C. 160), has "three offsets or procession-paths rising like steps one behind, and above the other, "but with no ornament now apparent, except a plain Buddhist rail of two bars on the outer "edge of the two lower ones, and an elephant cornice to the upper" . . . . "On each of the "four fronts of this dâgoba was an ornamental projection containing and partially concealing "the flights of steps by which access was had to these galleries."[1]

---

[1] *Ind. and East. Arch.*, p 190.

Another example at Mengûn, in Burma, has five ascending concentric procession-paths, each with niches for statues, and four flights of steps facing the four cardinal points.[1]

The temple at Boro Buddor in Java has five, in this case square, procession-paths around a central circular dâgoba. This building combines a vihâra with a dâgoba, in that the succession of statue niches in the different galleries, simulates the original cells for monks.[2] The fundamental principle is seen at another temple, Brambanam, in Java, which has a central shrine with sixteen (detached) shrines for statues around.[3] Another building, at Pollonarua, whatever its purpose may have been, has a plan which closely resembles that at Ghaṇṭaśâlâ, and may thus be also referred to. Mr. Fergusson in describing it, states, that "close to the Sat Mahal is a circular building, which, so far as "at present known, is unique. It may almost be described as a hollow dâgoba, being a circular "enclosure surrounded by a wall, but empty in the centre, at least containing nothing now. "Originally, it may have had a shrine in its centre or tabernacle of some sort, containing "a relic, or, more probably, a sacred Tree. It is surrounded by a procession-path, enclosed by "a highly ornamental screen, and beyond this by a second gallery adorned with a range of "slender pillars, like those which surround the dâgobas at Anuradhapura; below this, again, "is a richly-carved stylobate. Four flights of steps lead up to its procession-paths, more "magnificent and elaborate than any others that have yet been discovered in Ceylon."[4]

A comparison of the plan of the present building, with those above quoted, will show that it must belong to the same class. The inner circle forms the wall of the dome, stilted to the springing line at the level of the procession-path which surrounds it (pl. XIV, fig. 1). The breadth from the dome wall to the face of the outer brick ring is excessive for only one procession-path. The proportions would indicate two, in addition to the stylobate itself a procession-path. The facing wall of the upper offset would rise over the inner circumference of the broad outer ring. The two paths thus formed, are of similar breadth. They would probably have a parapet around the edge of each. The lower stylobate may also have had the same, or a row of slender pillars, as in one of the examples quoted from Ceylon. The relics are usually placed at the level of the procession-path. The approximate heights of these galleries would thus be fixed by the position of the relics in the relic chamber in the centre of the stûpa. The small chatti was found 3 feet from the surface of the mound. Its position would fix the level of the upper path and springing line of the dome. The bottom of the wide portion of the relic chamber, 10 feet below the top of it was from its shape, evidently intended for the reception of a relic. It would mark the height of the second gallery. The solid square in the centre of the building would be carried up, and form the thî over the dome summit. The walls of the hollow square chamber would support the rails of the enclosure, which sculptures represent around the thî. The approximate heights of the building may thus have been, 4 feet 6 inches to the level of the existing stylobate: a further height of 8 feet 6 inches to the second gallery, with the upper one 10 feet above it. If the dome were a semi-diameter, its height above the upper procession-path would equal 27 feet 11 inches, thus making its total height, exclusive of the thî, nearly 54 feet. The radiating walls outside the inner circle or assumed dome, may have been simply added to strengthen it, by preventing the great lateral thrust which would unavoidably take place in a dome of inferior brick construction thus stilted. That a lateral thrust has resulted, even

[1] *Ind. and East. Arch.*, p. 624.
[2] *Ibid.*, p. 646.
[3] *Ibid.*, p. 652.
[4] *Ibid.*, p. 203.

with these buttressing walls, is shown by its bulging out at parts. This latter fact itself strengthens the theory of this having been the dome wall. The radiating walls probably served a two-fold purpose, in that they also may have formed cells, or niches for statues as in the similarly constructed buildings above quoted. If these existed, they would open on to the second procession-path. The two cells opposite each of the four cardinal points are wider than those in the angles. Thus, room would be left for a sufficiently broad stair to pass up between them to the upper gallery, and yet leave their façades of the same width as that of the intermediate cells. Though, as at present existing, these cells are filled with packed mud, it must be remembered, that the walls only represent the foundations below the line of the gallery on to which the cells would open.

CHAPTER XIX.

OTHER REMAINS IN AND NEAR GHAṆṬAŚÂLÂ.

Bauddha-vanam, or Dharmakôṭa is an ancient site, now a piece of waste ground near the parchari on the extreme northern boundary of the village. Pits have been dug at places, by the villagers, for mud. In these holes are numbers of large bricks. Other antique objects are occasionally found by the diggers, but it is probable that in the majority of cases, nothing more is heard of them. Some time ago, a brass dîpa and a brass image of Śiva were found here. They are now in the Śiva temple at Ghaṇṭaśâlâ. A small triśula and a chakra were recently found on the same spot. These have all probably belonged to some Hindu shrine which once stood there. The dîpa (pl. XXXIII, fig. 2) is similar to many now in use in temples, for burning camphor before the image. It has a moulded base and bowl, each with a line of Telugu letters around it. These mention the name of a Chetti, one Uchchasettiyappa as the builder of the holy seat of the friend of Lakshmi, *i.e.*, Vishṇu. The lid to the bowl is hinged and perforated. A handle with a vyali's head in the middle, is fixed to the necking; its other end rests on a small circular base. The small Śaivite image is represented on plate XXXIV. The two small projections in the base are for affixing a canopy. Two holes below them are for the cords which bind the image to the vâhana, or other pedestal on which it is carried during processions. The head-piece is a curious one, and the bands around the knees are not usually seen on such images. Plate XXXIII (figs. 1 and 3) shows the triśula and chakra just referred to. Each is fixed on a pedestal, or hand grasp, moulded with alternate beads and hollows, and moulded base and capital. The chakra encloses a cross with cusps in the quadrants; these give it the appearance of a small runic cross.

REMAINS NEAR GHAṆṬAŚÂLÂ.

At the south-west of the parchari on the south boundary of the village, is a low mound named Polimêradibba. Some loose bricks appear on the surface of the mound, but it has been so much demolished, that the traces are not sufficient to show what building may have been there. Some marble piers from the stûpa are fixed on the mound as boundary posts. A few yards away, are some earth pits; these show courses of ancient brickwork at two feet from the surface.

On the south, just over the village boundaries, and situated within those of Dêvarakôṭa, is a low mound on the banks of a tank. It measures about seventy feet across, and is roughly circular in plan. The foundations of brick walls appear at places, and brick debris lie all over it. It may possibly be the remains of a stûpa.

Śrîkâkulam is a village in the Tsallâpalli Zamindâri, standing on the left bank of the Kṛishṇa river about nineteen miles west of Masulipatam. It is traditionally stated to be the site of the first capital of the Andhra dynasty.[1] The present village is entirely modern. There is a large temple, which is considered very sacred. The priests state that it was founded by Anantapâla, prime minister of Sumati Mahârâja, by whom is meant

[1] Burgess: *Amar. and Jagg. Stûpas*, p. 3.

ANCIENT PÛJA UTENSILS.

Fig. 1.

Fig. 2.

Fig. 3.

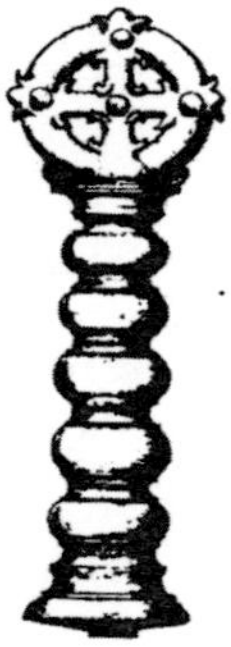

Scale of 12' 9' 6' 3' *Scale for Fig. 2.* 1 Foot.

Scale of 1' 2' 3' 4' 5' 6' 7' 8' 9' 10' 11' *Scale for Figs. 1 and 3.* 12 Inches.

Litho. S I O. Calcutta

Brass Image of Siva.

Scale of 0" 3" 6" 9" 12" Inches.

Photo, S. I. O., Calcutta.

Simuka, the first of the Andhra dynasty. No part of the present structure is so ancient. The earliest is the shrine, which dates from the 11th century. Later grants were made by the Vijayanagar kings and others. A large entrance gôpuram was built only a few years ago. In front of the temple is a large kulam or tank constructed by one of the Zamindârs of Dêvarakôṭa.

No traces of the ancient town are visible. It is stated to have been destroyed by the shifting of the river channel. Its site is now in the bed of the river. A temple of a much earlier date than the present one is stated to have stood there. Its ancient traditions may have been appropriated by the more modern shrine.

CHAPTER XX.

ANCIENT SITES IN THE RÊPALLE TALUK.

A catalogue of ancient mounds in the Kṛishṇa district was prepared by order of Government in 1889. Those in the Rêpalle taluk have been inspected, and notes of them are given below. The most of them are ancient village sites. Only a very few have remains of brick or stone buildings; thus showing that the houses had been constructed of mud. In general, only those mounds which show traces of buildings of interest should be dug into; as where these exist, they act as a guide where to dig, and may show whether objects of interest are likely to be found. The popular idea among the people of these districts, that mounds covering the remains of Buddhist buildings are store-houses of treasure, is a myth. These buildings, it is almost needless to say, were temples built to enshrine a relic, which also may have had placed along with it some articles of no great intrinsic value. Treasure would not, and never has been, found in such places; yet it is widely believed in. This idea is one of the causes which have led to the complete demolition of so many of these stûpas. It must have arisen through exaggerated accounts of golden or other relics which have been found inside them. The mound at Bhaṭṭiprôḷu was believed to contain five crores, the amount being estimated from the fact of a five-headed Nâga having once been discovered. The search for, and finding of the recently discovered relics, caused great interest among the people, even in distant villages; crowds came and visited the place, while the work was proceeding, and discussed the inscribed caskets after they were brought out. Most of those who were not present when the articles were brought to the surface went away convinced that a great treasure had just been dug out. There seems reason to believe that there is much treasure buried in the Kṛishṇa district, but it is in secret places, or in places which were once secret, but are now exposed. Such are the sites or foundations of houses which have become ruined or completely razed. These may be found by chance ploughing or digging as at Chaṇḍavôḷu, or, as with a find of Roman coins lately made. Numbers of small antique articles of interest must often be found by those digging into these village sites for earth, for brick-making or other purposes; but their finds are almost invariably kept secret. An instance is the small brass articles from Bauddhavanam at Ghaṇṭaśâlâ, which would never have been heard of, but for the coincident presence of the Survey.. The chances are, however, against anything that might be found in such sites repaying the outlay of a systematic search for it by digging. It is not under every house that treasure is buried; or, if so placed, that it is left there when the house is deserted or destroyed. In places where coins are found scattered about after rain, good results may be obtained by examining the earth with sieves.

ANANTAVARAM.

Fifteen miles north by west of Rêpalle. Yelûlapâḍu dibba is a piece of waste ground, over an acre in extent, among the fields on the south of the village. The soil is black mud, and has been extensively dug into for brick-making. The earth is thickly mixed with broken pottery and bones of animals. There are no traces of buildings visible on the surface, or in the pits dug by the brick-makers. It is an ancient village site.

BEZVÂDA.

Monolithic Jaina Column.

Scale of 12" 9" 6" 3" 0" 1 Foot.

Photo., S. I. O., Calcutta.

Bhattiprôḻu.

Before described.

Buddhâni.

Eighteen miles west by south of Rêpalle. Jains'dibba is the name given to an ancient village site, over a portion of which the present village is built. The soil is black mud, mixed with broken pottery. Several years ago some copper Buddhist images were found.[1] The spot pointed out is now cultivated as a garden. In it lies a plain white marble pier. Adjoining it is a piece of vacant ground, with a number of large circular pits dug all over it. Some of these are for storing grain, and others to supply earth for the fields. They have been dug to an extra depth in search of treasure; but nothing, so far as I can learn, was ever found. The earth is mixed with bricks and broken pottery.

Chaṇḍavôḻu.

Fifteen miles west of Rêpalle. A large mound on the north of the village, which it has been thought might cover the remains of some ancient building, is a Muhammadan burying ground; it is thickly covered with grave stones. No examination of what it may contain, can therefore be made. On the south of the village is a low mound running east and west for a quarter of a mile. It is known as Kôṭadibba, and is said to be the remains of a fort. Broken pottery and bricks are found when the earth is disturbed. When any digging is done by the roadside or in the house-yards of the village, pillars and other stones are occasionally turned up. An immense treasure in gold was found at some considerable depth underground when the canal was being cut. It was discovered by chance, as in most cases of treasure-finding; and had probably been buried under a house, which had become ruined and its site ploughed over. The masses of gold were in size and shape like-bricks; and were taken by the finders to be brass and sold as such in the bazaar. The *District Manual* (pp. 209, 210) states that gold coins are often found here.

Chaṇḍûru.

Nineteen miles north-west of Rêpalle. Uppala dibba is a small salt mound by the side of the village near the canal.

Koṇḍamuḍi.

Seventeen miles west by north of Rêpalle. In the centre of the village is a low open mound, measuring about 40 feet across and 6 feet high. It is surrounded by houses. Its section is seen at some places where it has been dug into. The earth is black mud, mixed with pottery, and layers of ashes at different levels. It forms the summit of the rising ground on which the village is built. About twenty years ago, the ground for some considerable space around it was of the same height, but the mud has gradually been removed from all sides for use on the fields, and the cleared ground built on. It is the last remaining portion of the higher ground of the ancient village site.

Maṇḍûru.

Fifteen miles north-west of Rêpalle. The Pati dibba is a low mound of black mud and broken pottery in the centre of the village. It measures about 150 feet across. It is an ancient village site.

---

[1] Sewell: *Topog. Lists of Antiq.*, vol. I, p. 78.

Môrakûru.

Eighteen miles north-west by west of **Rêpalle**. The **Kaṇḍepati dibba** is a deserted village site, covering about an acre of ground, half-a-mile to the south of the village. The earth is black mud, mixed with fragments of pottery. Copper, lead, and occasionally gold and silver coins are found after rain.

Mûlpûru.

Fourteen miles north-west of **Rêpalle**. The **Pati dibba** is a mound in the village similar to that at **Koṇḍamuḍi**.

Peravali.

Eleven miles north-west of **Rêpalle**. The **Jains' dibba** in the village, is a mound like that at **Mûlpûru**.

Pinapâḍu.

Nineteen miles north-west by north of **Rêpalle**. The **Mallipati dibba** is a deserted village site near the parchari on the south of the village. It is about a hundred yards square. It has been extensively dug into, for brick-making, and encroached on by the surrounding fields, so that its original extent must have been greater. The soil is that usually found on such sites. It is said 'that about three years ago,' some gold jewellery was found here, by some one who was removing earth for the roads.

CHAPTER XXI.

BUDDHIST MARBLE CARVING FROM AMARÂVATI.

The accompanying examples of antique carving, are copied from marbles now in the Madras Museum.

Though the fragmentary remaining portions of architecture, and sculpture, found at the Amarâvati stûpa, have been already represented in the published works of Drs. Fergusson and Burgess, in a manner well calculated to give an idea of their beauties, the necessarily small scale of the illustrations prevented various details of the carving being shown, sufficiently large, to be of service to architects or others, who might wish to use them for suggestions in design. Leaving out of mention the strictly sculptural subjects, a volume might be filled with choice bits of carving—perfectly suited for adaptation to a variety of purposes—taken from the Madras Museum marbles alone. Though such a work would not be without interest—as showing the diversity of design these sculptors found it possible to evolve from a few original forms—a limited selection may partly serve the same end. To an architect or designer, who desires to produce original work in an existing style, he can generally succeed, if he only has examples before him, sufficient to enable him to realize the feeling, which runs through it; or, grasp the guiding principles observable in its design.

Some specimens of varied floral carving, to illustrate the general style of this class of work, are here shown, on a scale sufficiently large for the purpose. A few of them appear in the plates of Dr. Burgess' work; the majority have not been published.

The class of art, found in the remains at Amarâvati, has been chiefly associated with that building; but, that the perfection in the sculptural arts, existing at this period in Southern India, was general among Buddhist workmen, and not confined simply to those working at this architectural masterpiece, is shown by examples identical in style, found at other buildings of the age, subsequently discovered. For a long time it was thought, that Amarâvati was the only building in its district which contained examples of such works. It had been asserted, in explanation of the existence of some marbles at places in other parts of the Kṛishṇa district, that they might have been removed—in some cases long distances—from that building. Later researches have, however, proved, that these others formed part of buildings which stood on the sites where they were found; and, that they had no such connection with Amarâvati. The Hindu, who places no value on anything architectural or sculptural which stands outside a consecrated temple, would be the last to think of removing any sculptures for their mere artistic value. When he did so, it was, on account of some fancied resemblance certain marble sculptures might bear to some of his objects of worship; or, he removed them, as he generally did, in the form of mortar.

To the Buddhists, we owe the introduction, not only of stone architecture into India, but of a class of sculpture that in parts partook of and rivalled the life-like representations of the Greeks. Sculpture was employed to an enormous extent in the embellishment of their temples; the most perfect examples seem to have been literally covered with it from base to summit. Floral carving occupied a subsidiary place; and is used as a setting to the sculptured panels, or to enrich the details of architecture.

With the expulsion of the Buddhists, there passed away a mastery of the sculptural arts, which, in India has never since been equalled. Sculptured groups represented the human figure true to nature, with none of the grotesque, distorted forms so freely adopted in the later works of the Hindus. The more antique ornament never asserts itself, but is always in subordination, and acts as an accessory to the feature to which it is applied. Some of the florid ornament of the later styles, is often applied contrary to its constructive use. On the other hand, though the later carved ornament of the Dravidians does not lack in beauty, it differs as much from the Buddhist as does the Roman from the Greek.

Early South Indian Buddhist sculpture is of a severely quaint character, and is generally in basso, while the later works, with their spirited life-like scenes, are in mezzo-relievo; the carved ornament of both periods is invariably in the former. The raised surface of the objects carved, is as flat as possible, with the edges only rounded off. This style of ornament, with its soft light and shade, does not detract from the solidity of any constructive object to which it is applied. The favourite floral representations are taken from the leaves, flowers, and buds of the sacred lotus. The flower readily lends itself to an infinity of varied grouping in the hands of a skilful carver. This, and the delicacy of treatment possible with the fine-grained material used, have been fully taken advantage of. The design is occasionally strictly conventional; though in some examples a free natural treatment, or a combination of the two is adopted. Other flowers than the lotus are often employed; and the incorporation of floral designs with different animals, grotesque and otherwise, always exhibits a strikingly artistic design with faultless execution.

Plate XXXVI.

The upper portion of a carved shaft, from one of the pilasters, which separated the chaitya slabs of the inner rail. The full pilaster is shown on plate XL, fig. 3, of Dr. Burgess' work on Amarâvati.[1] The shaft, as usual, supports a chakra, and is surrounded by clinging groups of figures. It has not been considered necessary to reproduce these here. It is divided in the height by a series of moulded and sculptured bands. The exposed sections of the shaft are in a flat semi-octagon, ornamented with twisted linear designs such as those shown.

Plate XXXVII.

Ornamental bands from the piers of the outer rail. They run along at the base of the piers, forming the lowermost portion of the carving. Fig. 1 is an arrangement of lotus buds; and fig. 2 a running floral pattern, with the details somewhat abraided. Fig. 3 shows a series of zig-zags, filled with tapering bands, like an arrangement of reeds. A somewhat similar design, in circular form, appears in the above work.[2] Fig. 4 is zig-zag with the triangles filled with a bead-and-leaf pattern.

Plate XXXVIII.

Three examples of the exterior bands on the circumference of panels of the outer rail. Fig. 1 shows cherubs at play with marine animals resembling the dolphin. One cherub rides astride the animal, while another is in the act of grappling one with a hook. Figs. 2 and 3 have a running pattern of the lotus, and animals, alternately.

---

[1] *Amar. and Jagg. Stûpas.* [2] *Ibid.*, pl. XVII, fig. 2.

Plate XXXIX.

The three figures in the plate are in continuation of each other; and represent a carved band, placed along the top of a coping stone from one of the earlier sculptures.[1] The principal flower is the lotus, in a natural arrangement of design. The carving is much frayed.

Plate XL.

Fig. 1 a band surrounding one of the circular discs carved on a pier of the outer rail. The design is a succession of pateras encircled by wreaths.

Fig. 2 is a fragment of a stone, evidently the base of a panel. It has a simple arrangement of lotus flowers and buds. The finer details are worn off.

Plate XLI.

Fig. 1 is a band, with foliage freely treated, from a sculptured coping panel of the outer rail.

Fig. 2 is a portion of a class of flat curved stones, described and illustrated by Dr. Burgess.[2]

Plate XLII.

Figs. 1 and 2 are the two portions of a band along the base of a pier of the outer rail. Some of these have a makara at each end, with foliage or animals between. This example has a makara on the left, with a lotus scroll on the remainder.

Plate XLIII.

The two portions of another specimen of the class of carved band above described.[3]

Plate XLIV.

Two portions of a band as above noted, with animals introduced among the foliage.[4]

Plates XLV and XLVI.

Other two examples of the same class.[5]

Plate XLVII.

Fig. 1 the lower portion of a sculptured panel from the outer rail. In the upper part of the panel are sculptured figures. The piece here shown is a representation of a tank with growing lotus plants, and birds standing in the water. Fig. 2, a fragment of a longitudinal panel, with a procession of hamsas.

---

[1] *Amar. and Jagg. Stûpas*, pl. xxix, fig. 3.

[2] *Ibid.*, p. 68, and pl. xxxi, fig. 2.

[3] *Ibid.*, pl. xi, fig. 4.

[4] *Ibid.*, pl. v, fig. 2.

[5] *Ibid.*, pl. v, fig. 1, and pl. vii, fig. 2.

APPENDIX.

The following note on the stones from the Bhaṭṭiprôḷu caskets, has been communicated by Dr. Warth, of the Madras Museum :

"As regards the Bhaṭṭiprôḷu relics, I have now closely examined the most important piece, the small phial which contains the three fragments of bone. The phial consists of a lightly greenish beryl crystal, hollowed out cylindrically and with a small perforation at the base.

"The crystal agrees with beryl in the following points :—

"1. Its light greenish color.

"2. Its specific gravity = 2·67.

"3. Its hardness ; it scratches quartz and is scratched by corundum.

"4. The form of crystallisation, as far as the artist allowed it to remain ; a prism of hexagonal section with an extra pair of faces(1).

"5. The polariscope examination. It being polished parallel to the base on both ends ; the tourmaline polariscope shows clearly through the section of $\frac{1}{6}$ inches thickness the uniaxial interference figure.

"6. There are also cracks parallel to the basal cleavage.

"The lid is a small piece of quartz crystal.

"That another smaller and more bluish crystal of casket No. 2 of the following size(2)———has been proved beryl by the most decisive observations of Professor Dr. Max Bauer of Marburg University, I told you before. He found the specific gravity 2·69, and found the uniaxial interference figure to show in a direction parallel to certain characteristic internal lines.

"Four more crystals in the other caskets leave no doubt that they are also beryls. One of them is a symmetrical regular hexagonal prism, and the other a stretched one with the exact angles. The sizes are(3)———.

"The three small amethysts, which are bored lengthways are easily recognized by their colour. Their sizes(4)———.

"There is a very small colorless quartz crystal, I should say, of this size and boring(5)———of round section. Then there are two pieces of coral, this size(6)———perforated lengthways.

"The few pearls have lost their lustre.

"The quartz crystal vases from 1 to 3 inches high of clear colorless quartz you know well, and the large inscribed hexagonal prism is also of quartz perforated lengthways.

"There is one small crystal this size(7)———of yellowish color perforated lengthways. This is probably only a yellow quartz, as I was able to scratch it with a topaz."

(1) See pl. vi. figs. 24 to 26.

(2) Pl. vi. fig. 16.

(3) Pl. vi. figs. 18, 19 and 29.

(4) Pl. vi. figs. 30 and 31 and pl. iv. fig. 10.

(5) Pl. vi. fig. 17.

(6) Pl. vi. fig. 20.

(7) Not illustrated.

AMARÂVATI.

BUDDHIST MARBLE CARVING.

Fig. 1.

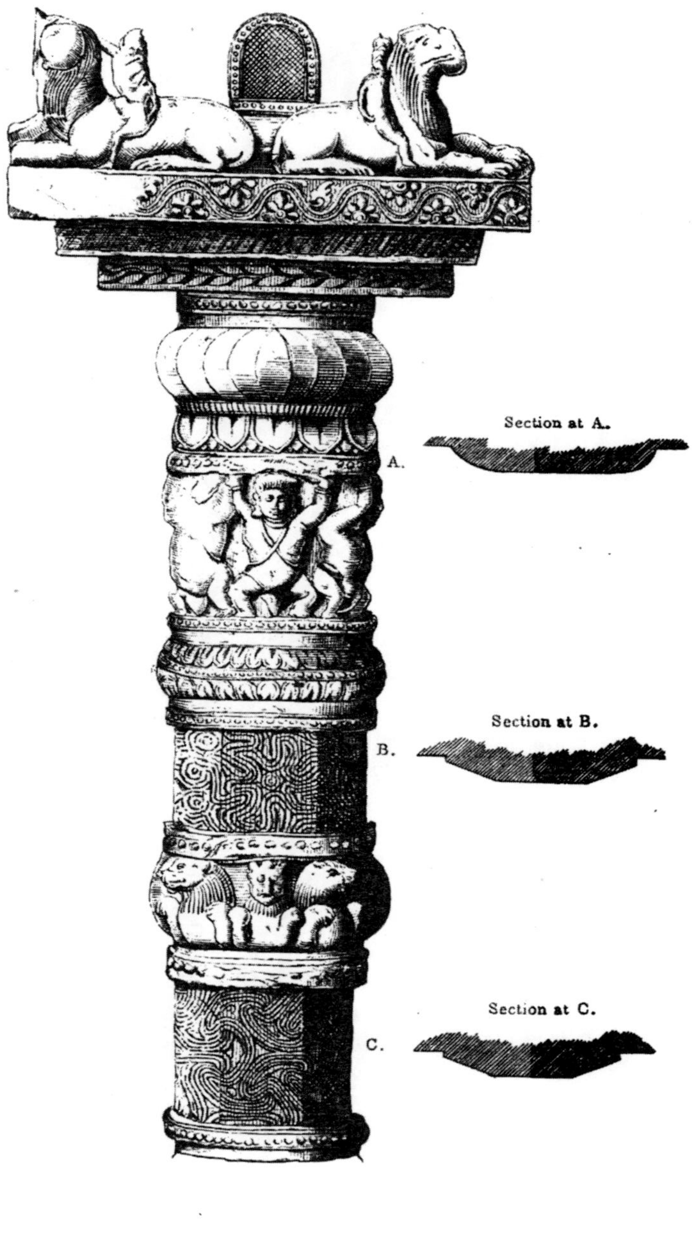

Scale of 1' 2' 3' 4' 5' 6' 7' 8' 9' 10' 11' 12 Inches.

Photo., S. I. O., Calcutta.

AMARÂVATI.

BUDDHIST MARBLE CARVING.

Fig. 1.

Fig. 2.

Fig. 3.

Fig. 4.

Scale of ⁚ 1 2 3 4 5 6 Inches.

Photo., S. I. O., Calcutta.

PLATE XXXVIII.

AMARÂVATI.

BUDDHIST MARBLE CARVING.

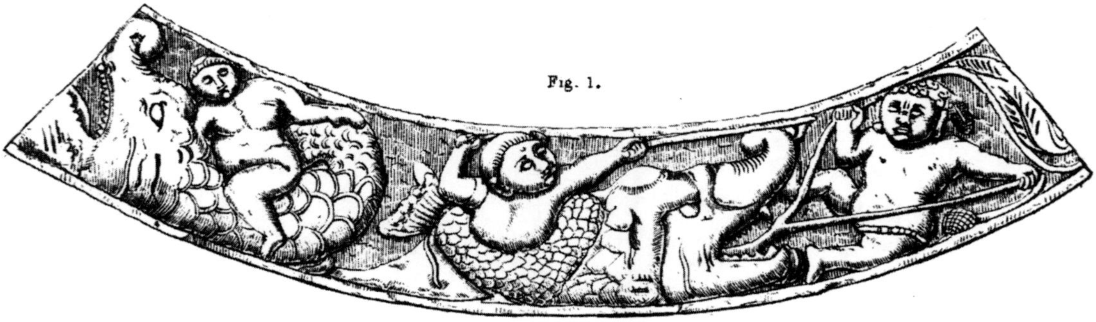

Fig. 1.

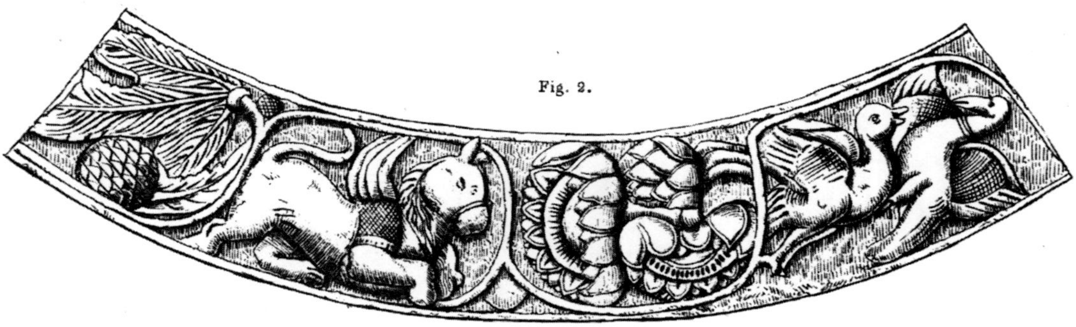

Fig. 2.

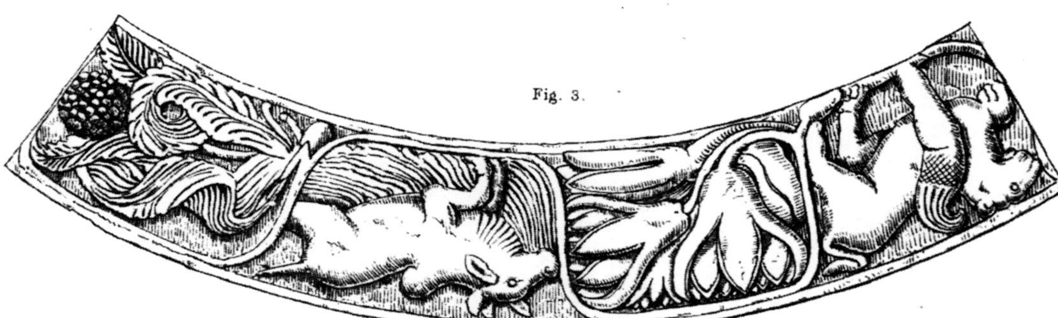

Fig. 3.

Photo. S. I. O. Calcutta.

AMARÂVATI.

BUDDHIST MARBLE CARVING.

Fig. 1.

Fig. 2.

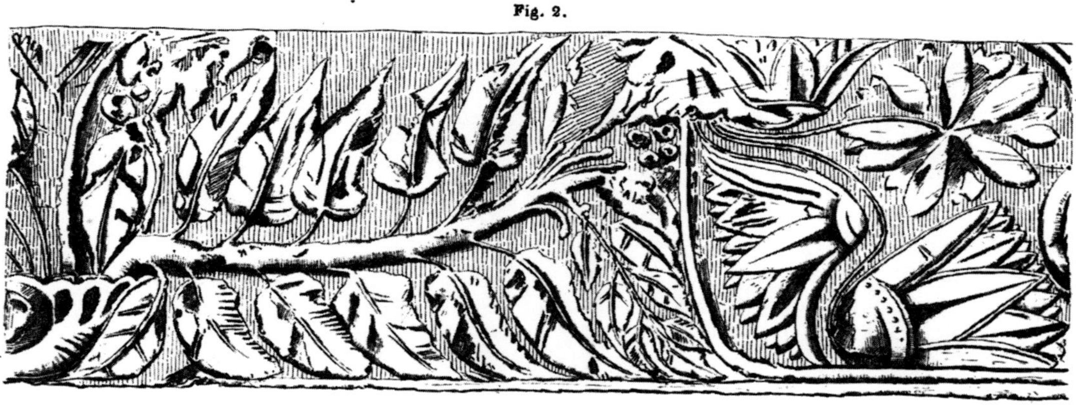

Fig. 3.

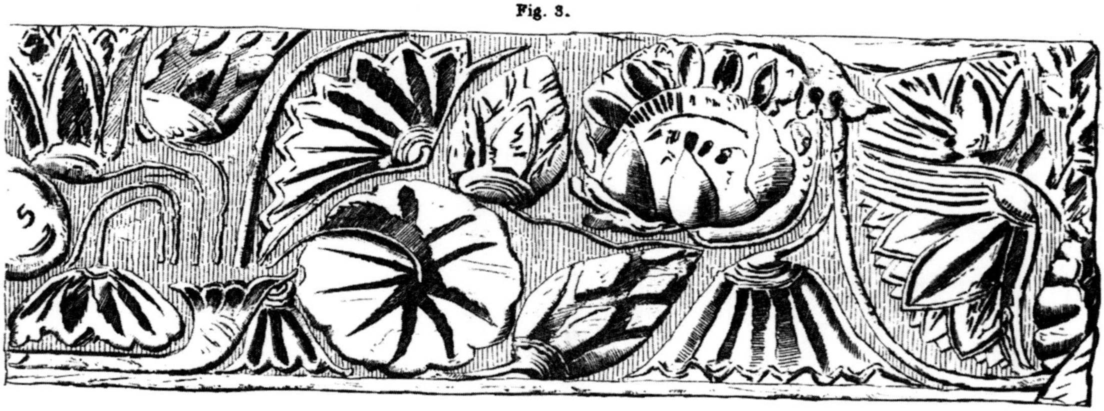

Scale of 0 1 2 3 4 5 6 Inches.

Photo., S. I. O., Calcutta.

AMARÂVATI.

Buddhist Marble Carving.

Fig. 1.

Fig. 2.

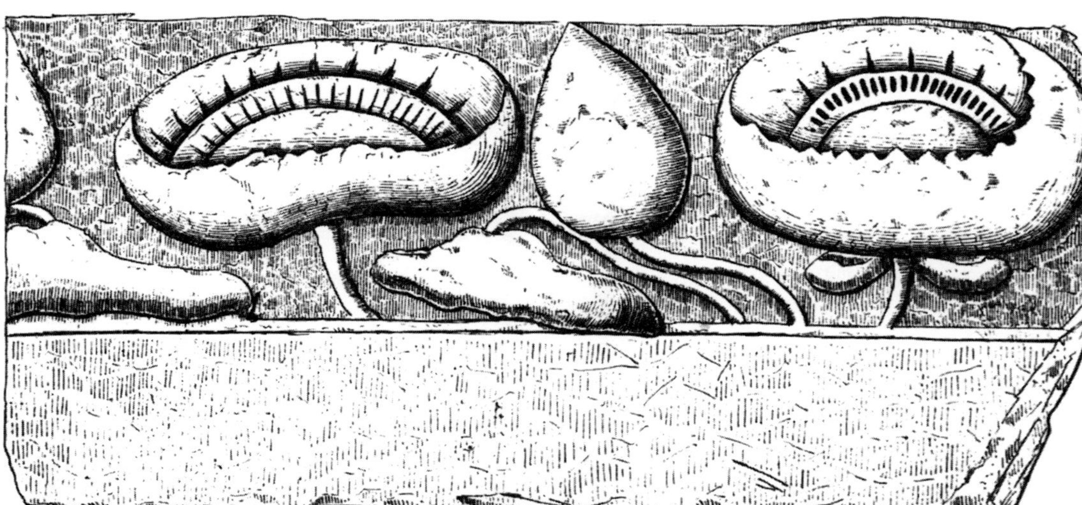

Scale of .: 1 2 3 4 5 6 Inches.

Photo., S. I. O., Calcutta.

AMARÂVATI.

BUDDHIST MARBLE CARVING.

Fig. 1.

Fig. 2.

Scale of .·. 1 2 3 4 5 6 Inches.

Photo., S. I. O., Calcutta.

AMARÂVATI.

BUDDHIST MARBLE CARVING.

Fig. 1.

Fig. 2.

Scale of . 1 2 3 4 5 6 Inches.

Photo., S. I. O., Calcutta.

AMARÂVATI.

BUDDHIST MARBLE CARVING.

Fig. 1.

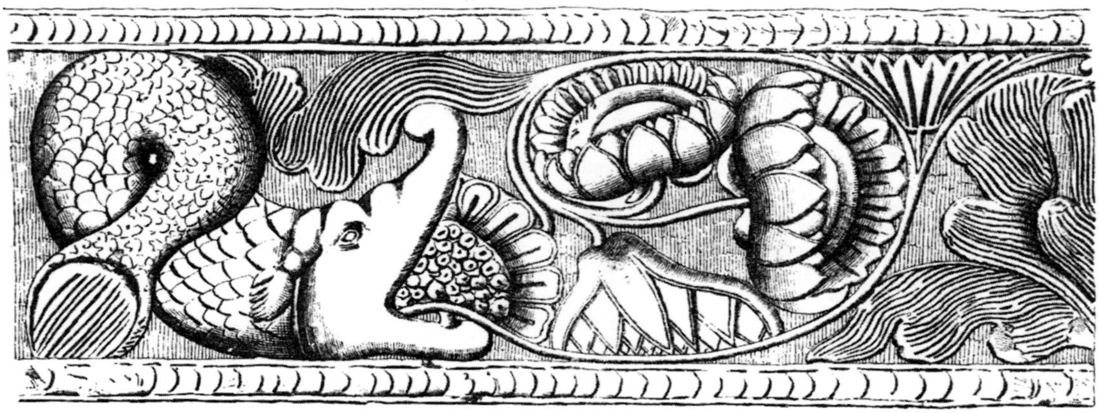

Fig. 2

Scale of ⁚ 1 2 3 4 5 6 Inches.

Photo. S. I. O., Calcutta.

AMARÂVATI.

BUDDHIST MARBLE CARVING.

Fig. 1.

Fig. 2.

Scale of 1 2 3 4 5 6 7 8 9 10 11 12 Inches.

Photo. S. I. O. Calcutta.

AMARÂVAṬI.

Buddhist Marble Carving.

Fig. 1.

Fig. 2.

Scale of . 1 2 3 4 5 6 Inches.

Photo., S. I. O., Calcutta.

AMARÂVATI.

BUDDHIST MARBLE CARVING.

Fig. 1.

Fig. 2.

Scale of .. 1 2 3 4 5 6 Inches.

Reg. No. 947, Arch., Madras.—Sep. 88.—350.

Photo., S. I. O., Calcutta.

BUDDHIST MARBLE CARVING.

Fig. 1.

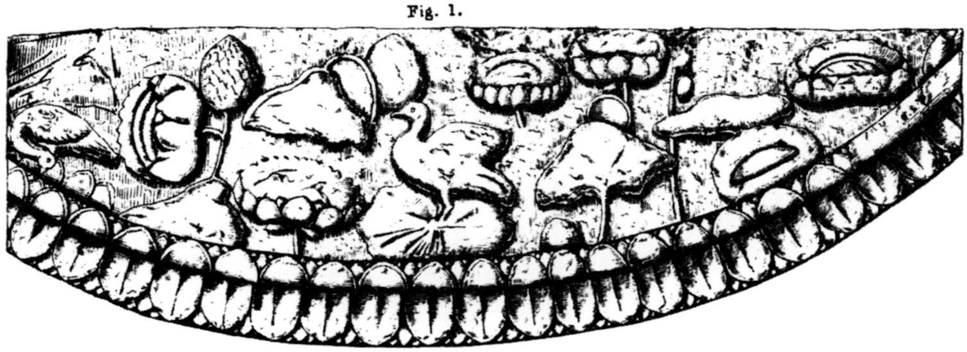

Fig. 2.

Scale of 1 2 3 4 5 6 Inches

Litho. S. I. O., Calcutta